FINDING A SOUL MATE
with
ASTROLOGY

FINDING A SOUL MATE
with
ASTROLOGY

LAURA ANDRIKOPOULOS

BALBOA PRESS
A DIVISION OF HAY HOUSE

Copyright © 2013 Laura Andrikopoulos.

All rights reserved. No part of this book may be used or reproduced by any means, graphic, electronic, or mechanical, including photocopying, recording, taping or by any information storage retrieval system without the written permission of the publisher except in the case of brief quotations embodied in critical articles and reviews.

Balboa Press books may be ordered through booksellers or by contacting:

Balboa Press
A Division of Hay House
1663 Liberty Drive
Bloomington, IN 47403
www.balboapress.com
1-(877) 407-4847

Because of the dynamic nature of the Internet, any web addresses or links contained in this book may have changed since publication and may no longer be valid. The views expressed in this work are solely those of the author and do not necessarily reflect the views of the publisher, and the publisher hereby disclaims any responsibility for them.

The author of this book does not dispense medical advice or prescribe the use of any technique as a form of treatment for physical, emotional, or medical problems without the advice of a physician, either directly or indirectly. The intent of the author is only to offer information of a general nature to help you in your quest for emotional and spiritual well-being. In the event you use any of the information in this book for yourself, which is your constitutional right, the author and the publisher assume no responsibility for your actions.

Any people depicted in stock imagery provided by Thinkstock are models, and such images are being used for illustrative purposes only.
Certain stock imagery © Thinkstock.

Printed in the United States of America

ISBN: 978-1-4525-6739-6 (sc)
ISBN: 978-1-4525-6741-9 (hc)
ISBN: 978-1-4525-6740-2 (e)

Library of Congress Control Number: 2013901138

Balboa Press rev. date: 1/22/2013

ALSO BY
LAURA ANDRIKOPOULOS:

Short Guides to Serious Astrology: Beginnings
Short Guides to Serious Astrology: Birth Chart Case Studies
Short Guides to Serious Astrology: Transits
Short Guides to Serious Astrology: Forecasting Your Year
Short Guides to Serious Astrology: Relationships
Short Guides to Serious Astrology: Fate
Understanding your Moon-sign

Contents

Part 1 - Preliminaries

    Chapter 1 - The Formula 3

    Chapter 2 - Your unique astrological chart. 6

Part 2 - Being True to Yourself

    Chapter 3 - Journeying through life 17

    Chapter 4 - Developing Your Heart Centre 26

    Chapter 5 - Understanding your emotional needs . . . 36

    Chapter 6 - Understanding your greatest fears 53

    Chapter 7 - Your key developmental path 71

    Chapter 8 - Assembling your unique True Self profile . 85

Part 3 - Understanding your relationship needs

    Chapter 9 - Your partnership sign 99

    Chapter 10 - Your style of relationship 108

    Chapter 11 - The Place of the Other 137

    Chapter 12 - Return to the Moon 145

Chapter 13 - Assembling your unique Relationship Needs profile 154

Part 4 - Putting it All Together

Chapter 14 - Calling your soul-mate 161

Chapter 15 - Happy Ever After? 168

Part 1

Preliminaries

In part one we will be discussing the formula for finding a soul-mate with astrology, and then outlining the main tool we will be using to do this: your unique astrological chart.

Chapter 1

The Formula

Finding a soul-mate is easier than you think! This book will give you a method and system to work with in order to do just that. And believe it or not, there is even a formula, which will be revealed to you below.

The matter is really quite simple. It is simple because the universe works in a particular way; there are spiritual laws governing its operation. The most important law for our purposes can be summarised as follows:

The universe is a huge vibrating energy system and you attract people and things into your life based on your energy frequency. When you are vibrating at your highest level, totally in tune with your real self, you easily attract the perfect partner for this particular stage of your life.

The question then becomes, how can I reach my highest level

of vibration, and how can I become my true self? To some extent this is a lifetime's work, as we are all on a journey of spiritual progress and growth. However, life has given us a wonderful tool in which to learn our true nature more easily: this tool is astrology.

Forget the simplistic twelve-sign columns you see in popular newspapers and magazines. Such columns have their place as a very broad and general system of divination, but they are just the tip of the iceberg when it comes to the real knowledge astrology has to offer you.

The astrological chart is a highly complex map, totally unique and personal to you, laying out your inner dynamics. It is a fascinating world of personal exploration, and if you work creatively with the knowledge contained within it, you can expand and improve your life immensely.

One of the greatest gifts of astrology is that it helps you understand who you really are. The most successful relationships are based on two adults coming together as equals, each fully themselves and able to exist without the other. When each person is being true to themselves and their nature, they are able to relate to another in the cleanest possible manner.

Being happy with yourself, feeling that you are on the road to fulfilment, that you are able to express yourself as you really are, is the absolute best place from which you can conduct a relationship with another human being. Astrology helps you align with your true self. In this state you are in the perfect position to receive the abundance of the universe. Such abundance includes a loving relationship; a soul-mate.

Astrology also has a great deal to say on what you need in a relationship. Thus, in addition to providing invaluable wisdom on your own path to fulfilment, it also suggests the sort of connections that will please and honour your being. Whilst part two of this book will concentrate on your own nature and needs as shown by astrology, the third part will consider what your chart might say about your requirements of a relationship.

Part four will conclude the process of finding a soul-mate, bringing all the knowledge you have gathered together so far and discussing how you might then attract in your perfect partner. It will also discuss questions such as whether relationships last forever and whether you can be happy without any partner at all.

We can now summarise the formula for finding a soul-mate:

1. Become as happy and fulfilled as you possibly can be through using astrological knowledge

2. Understand your real relationship needs as shown by astrology

3. Collate your knowledge and call in your soul-mate

Sounds simple, doesn't it? It is!—if you are willing to do the work and follow the guidance that you find.

Throughout the book you will also be encouraged to consider your intuitive guidance, and pay attention to any signs and symbols you receive from the universe. Life is a rich, unfolding and quite magical journey, if you let it be.

CHAPTER 2

YOUR UNIQUE ASTROLOGICAL CHART

THIS BOOK DOES NOT ASSUME an advanced knowledge of astrology; it is designed for those who have an interest beyond Sun-signs (sometimes known as 'Star signs') and are prepared to work with their chart. If you have a copy of your chart and know what planets you have in which signs and houses that is a great start. If you do not, then the information below will aid you in finding your chart.

You can obtain your full birth chart from a number of free websites on the Internet. The best such website to do so is www.astro.com. You will need to add in your details to the 'My Astro' section; the data required is your time, date and place of birth in addition to basic information such as your name and sex. Then go to the 'Free Horoscopes' section and select personal portrait. At the bottom of this mini-reading you will find a list of your major planetary placements. What you require is something that looks like the following:

- » Sun in Scorpio in the 10th house
- » Moon in Libra in the 9th house
- » Mercury in Libra in the 8th house, and so on.

If you have any difficulty locating the data you need to gain the most from this book, you are welcome to contact me through my website www.starpoetry.co.uk. Just send me proof of purchase of the book, along with your birth date, time and location and I will provide you with what you need.

In this chapter we will outline some of the factors that make up an astrological chart so that you may begin to understand your own unique mandala, meaning a symbolic pattern personal to you. We will be focusing on the ones that are of prime importance in the quest for a soul-mate.

An astrological birth chart basically consists of three factors: planets or points, signs of the zodiac, and houses (areas of life). You will see that each planet or point is placed in a particular sign and a particular segment of the chart. The planets may be considered the fundamental building block of astrology. Before we consider these and other factors however, we will briefly review the signs of the zodiac.

Many people are familiar with zodiac signs, although their meanings are often popularised to an extent where their serious essence has been lost. The signs are twelve basic energies of life; to give you a flavour of their essential nature the following associations might prove useful:

- » Aries—initiation, action, adventure
- » Taurus—preservation, beauty, stability

- » Gemini—inquisitiveness, lightness, sociability
- » Cancer—nurturing capacity, imagination, sensitivity
- » Leo—pride, faith, drama
- » Virgo—analysis, focus, detail, integrity
- » Libra—balance, justice, harmony
- » Scorpio—intensity, transformation, emotional depth
- » Sagittarius—journey, the bigger picture, meaning, exploration
- » Capricorn—realism, pragmatism, mastery, achievement
- » Aquarius—principles, humanity, compassion, equality
- » Pisces—holism, escapism, inspiration

The signs will be important as we consider how the planets are placed in your chart, for each has a particular sign. For now, we will introduce the planets relevant to our task of finding a soul-mate.

The Sun, symbolised on the chart by a circle with a dot in it, represents your heart centre. It is your inner light, the creative self that longs to shine and be admired. This is the planet that principally connects with a sense of vocation, or calling. This shows what you were born to do and what area of life you will find most fulfilling to explore.

The Sun is an extremely important planet in the chart. It leads and provides the centre around which all others must function. It is also representative of key male figures such as husband and father, and can therefore say much about how we relate to the men in our life. We will discuss your particular Sun placement in chapter four.

The Moon, counterpart to the Sun, is our instinctual self,

our private self. Her symbol in astrological charts is the crescent Moon. She represents our habits and day to day existence. Her placement in the chart shows how we need to nurture and nourish ourselves. She symbolises the ebb and flow of our feelings and emotional life.

The Moon is another extremely important planet in the chart. Failing to feed your needs and give yourself the nurturing you require can lead to many problems. Fundamentally, if our Moon is not supported and honoured, we do not feel right with ourselves or the world. We will discuss how to nourish your own particular Moon in chapter five and how this placement may relate to relationships in chapter twelve. The Moon may also relate to your experience of mother and other important females in your life that provided some form of nurturing. Patterns of early parenting may replay in our adult relationships and as such this is also a key issue in terms of becoming aware of your astrological Moon and how you might be responding to life based on earlier patterns of conditioning rather than from your adult needs.

Venus is the planet of relationships and values and her symbol is the universal feminine icon. You should be able to spot her easily in your chart. She loves to associate with others, to be friendly and sociable. She enjoys the pleasure of interaction and the courtly side of romantic engagement. In the birth chart she gives a sense of those things we value in partnership, and the style of relationship that we will best flourish in. We will be discussing your own Venus in chapter ten as part of the focus on what you need and enjoy within partnership.

Saturn is an extremely important planet in astrology and his symbol looks like a cross with a curly tail to one side. He is the planet of initiation and true spiritual progress. He brings lessons and tests, but helps you to evaluate how you are progressing on your own unique journey thus far. Saturn is a very serious planet, and can be a hard teacher, but he is also full of wisdom.

The placement of Saturn in the birth chart shows an area of life that is immensely important to us. It can be a place however of fear, where we are sensitive to failure or public criticism. Overcoming any fears in the area of life that Saturn indicates through his placement in the chart is extremely rewarding. Wherever Saturn is suggests a place where you can achieve mastery and a real sense of achievement, once initial fears have been overcome.

Saturn is very important for our self-development. Once we have mastered Saturn, we are on the path of growth and maturity. He is essential for our own sense of fulfilment, and is a counterpart to the Sun in that sense. As we develop our Saturn, we develop a relationship with our incarnation here on Earth. This is our essential task here. Therefore, although on the surface Saturn may not seem to have much to do with relationships, he is vital in that he aids us in becoming more fully ourselves. From this state we are in a much better position to attract in a mature and serious connection with another person. We will be exploring your Saturn placement in chapter six.

The Sun, Moon, Venus and Saturn are the only planets we will be considering in this book as essential for the finding a soul-mate process. The other planets will however have brief mention in chapter eleven, when we discuss the house of relationships, which is the seventh area of a birth chart, and which relates to partnership.

Apart from the planets, there are other factors in astrology of great importance. These are the Moon's nodal axis, the angles of the chart, and the houses. We will look at the factors we need from each of these for our soul-mate quest below.

The Moon's nodal axis is a plane of intersection of the paths of Sun and Moon. It combines your path to fulfilment with your essential emotional nature. It is therefore an extremely potent factor in astrology, associated with personal growth, and fate and destiny themselves. This axis has two ends, called the North and South Nodes. The South Node shows where we have come from; it may relate to past lives or to qualities that come very easily to us. The North Node shows where we are going; it is a key point for our personal growth and relates to our destiny in this lifetime. We will be discussing your North and South Nodes in chapter seven.

The angles of a birth chart are the four points that represent the ends of the horizontal and vertical axes running through the chart. They are often in thicker type than the other spokes of the wheel to emphasise their importance. The axis we will be focusing on is the horizontal one. This is the Ascendant-Descendant axis.

The Ascendant is the sign of the zodiac that was rising on the eastern horizon at the time or your birth. It is shown by the sign on the left hand side of the chart and is often labelled 'ASC' or similar. This is a very important sign for you. It shows many fundamental qualities about you and the journey that you will make in life. It is rarely the same sign as your Sun-sign, although it can be. So this may be a sign that is new to you. We will be examining your Ascendant sign in chapter three.

The Descendent is always the zodiac sign opposite the one on the Ascendant. It represents the qualities that are furthest away from your natural self, and can therefore be what you try to seek in another person. Relationships are often attempts to complete ourselves, to find the missing half. This is why the qualities represented by the Descendant sign can be descriptive of the type of partner that is attractive to us. We will be examining your Descendant sign in chapter nine.

From your birth chart you will see that the chart is split into twelve different areas or segments; these are called the houses. They denote different areas of life and show where a planet will express itself most strongly. The houses each have a different meaning; the basic meanings are as follows:

- House One—how you approach life, how you begin things, basic personality traits
- House Two- your sense of self-value, your finances and earning power
- House Three—your local environment, siblings, matters concerning communication
- House Four—home, family, father, inner self
- House Five- creativity, children, self-expression
- House Six—daily routines, work, health, mind/body connection
- House Seven—relationships and partnerships
- House Eight—shared emotional and financial exchange, transformation, intimacy
- House Nine—worldview, philosophy, higher thinking
- House Ten—career, public status, mother
- House Eleven—friends, groups, community
- House Twelve—dreams, the unconscious, the all, dissolution

As we have already noted, house seven is particularly important to the concerns of this book, and we shall discuss this house in chapter eleven. We will however be looking at your Sun, Moon, Venus, Saturn and Nodes through the astrological houses so the meanings of all houses are relevant to our project.

We have now been introduced to the astrological factors that will support us in our journey to find a soul-mate. All astrological factors have positive purpose. Astrology is a system of guidance; it is ancient wisdom to help you navigate your life. We live in a good, loving universe full of signs to aid us on our individual quests. Astrological signs (in general, not just the zodiac signs) are particularly complex and rich ones, so make the best use of them and follow their guidance with pure intention.

Let our journey begin!

Part 2

Being True to Yourself

This section of the book will focus on the absolute core knowledge to be obtained from your astrological chart. It will extract information based on simple sign and house positions of key planets and points. By using this guidance to further your own happiness in life, with or without a partner initially, you greatly increase the chance of meeting someone suitable for you. The happier you are as an individual, and the more fulfilled on your life's journey, the more likely it is that you will attract in someone who matches you on the highest possible level.

Chapter 3

Journeying Through Life

OUR BASIC APPROACH TO LIFE and major themes in our life journey are shown by the zodiac sign of our Ascendant. In this chapter we shall consider each of these signs in turn. Find your own Ascendant sign and read the section relevant to you. Remember our overall goal in using this information is to improve our own life and to align with our true selves, so that we are then in an optimal state in which to meet a soul-mate. Work alongside your astrological energies, and you will be living in harmony with the cosmos. Your destiny will then unfold as it should, which includes meeting a suitable soul-mate.

Ascendant in Aries

With Aries rising you may view the world as a place to conquer. Life is about action and adventure. You are the archetypal hero, loving to set out on a new quest. You may begin things with great dynamism and enthusiasm, although this can quickly wear off.

The greatest strengths of your nature are your courage, passion and protectiveness towards those that need a strong presence beside them; cultivating these qualities will enhance your natural gifts.

The more difficult side of this rising sign may be in seeing the world as a place where you must fight and demand what you want, without thought for others. Try not to jump into things too hastily with a combative attitude.

Your life's journey will involve dealing with issues of assertion and of being a pioneer. Take these challenges head-on, as befits your forthright nature.

Ascendant in Taurus

Taurus on the Ascendant suggests that you see the world as a place that needs to be tackled in practical terms, brick by brick and stone by stone. You are a wonderful builder in every sense of the word. You gradually increase your sense of security in the world. Your nature is basically peaceful and placid.

The greatest strengths of your nature are your tranquillity and stability, plus your appreciation of the realm of the senses. Cultivating these qualities will enhance your natural gifts.

The more difficult side of this rising sign may be stubbornness and inflexibility. Try to accept change when it becomes necessary and let go of tightly held opinions when the time is right.

Your life's journey will involve dealing with possessions and holding on to things; you will be asked to build something of lasting, tangible value. Embrace your journey carefully and slowly, as befits your placid nature.

Ascendant in Gemini

Gemini rising gives an outlook of youth and vibrancy. You are butterfly like in your interests and have a light, inquisitive view onto the world. Intellectual and social stimulation are very important to your path through life and you benefit from new interests or courses of study.

Your greatest strengths are your quickness, wit and your versatility. Cultivating these qualities will enhance your natural gifts.

The more difficult side of this rising sign can manifest as scattered energy, when you have so many things on the go that you do not know where to begin and hardly achieve anything. You may always have more than one path to follow, but keep it to two, and no more!

Your life's journey will involve dealing with duality and embracing two paths at the same time; you may be challenged on matters to do with communication. Your innate flexibility and curiosity will aid you in working through your life tasks.

Ascendant in Cancer

Cancer on the Ascendant suggests an approach to life that is imbued with sensitivity and imagination. You are timid and like the crab hide inside your shell until you are sure it is safe to come out.

Your greatest strengths are your ability to nurture and empathise with others. You also have the ability to tune in to the feeling tone of different situations and respond appropriately. Cultivating these qualities will enhance your natural gifts.

The more difficult side of this rising sign can manifest as hypersensitivity and fearfulness over making new starts in life.

Try to build a thicker skin when it comes to receiving criticism and to think carefully through any irrational fears.

Your life's journey will challenge you on issues of home, mother, family and nurturing. Explore your relationship with your mother and family of origin, as the domestic past can loom large for this sign on the Ascendant.

Ascendant in Leo

With Leo rising, life is a stage and you were born to be at the centre of it. You have a natural love of drama and show and may approach life with generosity and faith. Being creative and self-expressive is important to your nature.

Your greatest strengths are your faith, warmth and generosity. You may light up a room with your bright presence, as you shine and display your innate confidence. Cultivating these qualities will enhance your natural gifts.

The more difficult side of this rising sign may be a tendency to play the drama queen! You may also become caught up in your own unique self and lose the ability to see others around you or your place in a group. Remembering your connection to other people and wider society can help to balance any such tendency.

Your life's journey may ask you to deal with issues around creativity and living from your heart. Approaching life from a joyful sense of faith, without over-naivety, can aid you in your path.

Ascendant in Virgo

Virgo rising suggests a careful, analytical approach to life. You may like to take small steps forward, digesting each chunk of experience before you proceed further. This sign gives a great deal of intelligence in applied knowledge and you are able to manifest your ideas in the world.

Your greatest strengths are your modesty, integrity and diligence. Cultivating these qualities will help to bring out your natural gifts.

The more difficult side of this rising sign can be a tendency to over-critique people or situations in your life, to become too fussy and focused on small details which do not necessarily matter. Trying to see the bigger picture will help to balance these traits.

Your life's journey may ask you to deal with issues surrounding the mind-body connection, and the proper digestion and dissection of your experience. Analysing carefully and calmly will help you meet these tasks with ease.

Ascendant in Libra

With Libra on the Ascendant you approach life with charm, grace and balance. You love to weigh up the pros and cons of decisions and to be seen as fair and just. You have a natural style and rationality when it comes to new beginnings.

Your greatest strengths are your sense of justice, your diplomacy and your natural charm. Cultivating these qualities will enhance your natural gifts.

The more difficult side of this rising sign can be a tendency to sit on the fence, to procrastinate and not take action for fear of confrontation or conflict. Well-planned out strategic moves may help you overcome any such tendency.

Your life's journey may challenge you on issues of justice and fairness. Weigh up each side as you strive to achieve the perfect balance.

Ascendant in Scorpio

With Scorpio rising you approach life from a deep viewpoint. You see the depth in everything and you are instinctively aware of the underlying motivations of the people around you. You may need to be somewhat ruthless in walking your life's path but you are also highly sensitive.

The greatest strengths of your nature are your emotional depth and your ability to withstand crisis and trauma. Cultivating these qualities will enhance your natural gifts.

The more difficult side of this rising sign can be a suspicious or paranoid streak that stops you reaching out and trusting others. As emotional engagement will be deeply fulfilling for you, this is something to be aware of.

Your life's journey may contain clear phases, in which endings and beginnings are clearly demarcated. You may have to deal with crises or difficult subjects but you have the natural resources to handle this. Keep walking your intense path and you will find your way through.

Ascendant in Sagittarius

Sagittarius rising brings life as a journey to the fore. You value your vast range of experiences along life's highway and are forever in search of meaning and the bigger picture. You are confident and have wide interests. There may be something about you that is larger than life and you need to be expanded on all levels in order to feel you are making progress.

Your greatest strengths are your optimism and vision for the future. You are able to find meaning and connect the dots to present the bigger picture. Cultivating these qualities will enhance your natural gifts.

The more difficult side of this rising sign can be forgetting the details of everyday life and being so focused on the future that you forget the now. Try to stay present with your life as it is and appreciate some of the more mundane aspects of existence.

Your life's journey may forever be a journey! For you the journey is more important than the final destination. You may be challenged on issues of faith and religion; tackle such questions with your broad intellect and far-seeing vision.

Ascendant in Capricorn

With Capricorn rising, life can seem a harsh and difficult place to be, a wasteland that has to be traversed. This can be a tricky sign to live rising but you make steady progress in life if you keep your self-confidence up and keep going. Eventually you are someone who can achieve great things with continual hard work.

Your greatest strengths are your realism and ability to deal with things as they actually are. Cultivating these qualities will enhance your natural gifts.

The more difficult side of this rising sign can be pessimism and a sense of the difficulty and struggle of existence. Keep going when all seems tough and eventually you will break out of the clouds into the sunshine.

Your life's journey may challenge you on issues of achievement, mastery and worldly success. You may also be given duties and responsibilities that must be fulfilled. Embrace your burdens as they may contain hidden treasure.

Ascendant in Aquarius

Aquarius rising suggests an approach to life that is detached, even scientific in a sense. You are open-minded, progressive and a natural humanitarian. You may rationalise your experience of life and have a keen sense of social justice.

Your greatest strengths are your compassion, humane attitude and ability to live from wider principles. Cultivating these qualities will enhance your natural gifts.

The more difficult side of this rising sign is over-detachment and impersonality which may create problems relating to others on an individual level. Remembering each person is unique and honouring them in this respect can help to balance any such tendency.

Your life's journey may challenge you on being progressive and different to other people in how you approach things. Embrace the chance to stand up for your principles and do what you believe in.

Ascendant in Pisces

With Pisces rising, life can seem chaotic and confusing. You approach life with great intuition and compassion but may struggle with being practical or keeping your feet on the ground. A natural mystic, you may love to escape to a fantasy realm.

Your greatest gifts are your intuition, your natural mysticism and your love of glamour and fantasy. Cultivating these qualities will enhance your natural gifts.

The more difficult side of this rising sign is the tendency to indulge in escapist activities which could take you on the path of drink or drugs. Developing spiritual or inspirational interests, or indulging in drama or virtual reality games, could help to deal with any such problems.

Your life's journey may challenge you on who you really are. With Pisces rising you have a chameleon-like quality. Staying centred and focused on your individuality will assist you as you walk through life.

Each rising sign says something about our fundamental personality. Living the highest qualities of our Ascendant puts us in touch with a profound part of our nature and helps us prepare for our soul-mate meeting.

Chapter 4

Developing Your Heart Centre

As we have already learned, the best way to attract your soul-mate is to put yourself in the highest possible state of alignment with who you really are. Your heart centre is a very important part of this and is symbolised in astrology by the placement of the astrological Sun.

When you hear people saying 'I am a Taurus' or 'I am a Gemini' the actual meaning of this is that the Sun was placed in the tropical zodiac sign of Taurus or Gemini when they were born. Thus, it is likely you already know what sign symbolises your heart centre. The other important information as regards your Sun are its house and the connections it is making to other planets. In this book, designed for those without extensive knowledge of astrology, we will be focusing on the sign and house placements only.

We briefly introduced the Sun in chapter 2 but we will review here in a little more depth what the Sun actually represents. The astrological Sun is symbolic of the absolute core of your being and identity; it shows what you need to do and be in order to find fulfilment and creative happiness. Think of the bright Sun in the sky warming the land and people beneath, shining with joy and light. This is how your inner spiritual Sun should be. The Sun is a delicate planet in astrological terms; if it is not nurtured and warmed by your cultivation of its qualities, it might easily descend behind a cloud. If you are feeling depressed or out of touch with yourself, it may be that you are not honouring your Sun in the way you should be.

At a simple level, the way in which we honour our Sun in terms of basic expression is to cultivate those qualities that the sign within which it is placed represents. Look up your own Sun-sign below to see the qualities you should strive to place at the centre of your life in order to find fulfilment.

Sun in Aries: cultivate initiation, independence and action. Ensure you are not dependent on others, and are free to do your own thing, with zest and enthusiasm for life. Start that project you have been meaning to for so long—take a leap of faith!

Sun in Taurus: cultivate stability and beauty in your life. Ensure you have savings for a rainy day, and have firm foundations from which to develop your interests. Take care to develop the things you already have in life, for preservation is a key concept in your nature and one that brings fulfilment.

Sun in Gemini: cultivate flexibility and a variety of interests. Take those courses that seem so fascinating, get out into the community to socialise with others. Develop your ability to communicate and exchange with others.

Sun in Cancer: cultivate your imagination and feeling. Take on a creative project which allows you to nurture it and tenderly bring it to fruition. Ensure that you have people in your life that you feel you are able to care for, even if it is at a distance. Whether male or female you have the energy of a 'mother figure' and developing a protective and nurturing identity is highly fulfilling.

Sun in Leo: cultivate creativity and drama in your life. Allow yourself that bit of panache and showing off. Join that drama group you have been interested in for so long. Take up that activity that makes you feel special and important amongst others. Honour your heart above all things.

Sun in Virgo: cultivate discernment and efficiency. Allow yourself to work methodically and diligently, building up a reputation as a hard worker with great integrity. Develop your analytical skills and your sense of what is right and wrong for you. Carefully digest experience so that you gradually, step by step, grow into a stronger sense of being.

Sun in Libra: cultivate balance and harmony in your life. Seek out justice and a role that allows you to play the arbiter or diplomat. Develop your role as a peacemaker and a bridge between opposing factions. Allow yourself to live with grace and style.

Sun in Scorpio: Cultivate your depth and emotional engagement with life. Allow yourself to feel deeply and involve yourself with matters of the utmost importance. See crisis as an opportunity for you to test your mettle, for you will find yourself most clearly when you are tested in extreme situations. You will grow a powerful identity through involving yourself in all that lies beneath the surface.

Sun in Sagittarius: Cultivate freedom and vision in your life. Find a path and follow it with all your heart. Search for a meaning by which you can live. Imagine the future and develop your optimistic side so that you can almost taste and feel your success.

Sun in Capricorn: Cultivate responsibility and mastery. Continue with whatever really touches you, even when it is hard work. Keep climbing the mountain even when the way forward seems dark, and you cannot see beyond the wasteland. Develop your hardworking nature and welcome the authority that will naturally accrue to you.

Sun in Aquarius: Cultivate equality and compassion. Develop your interest in politics and society; get involved with the groups that capture your attention. Allow yourself to be as independent and different as you want to be. Follow your compassion and concern for all humanity.

Sun in Pisces: Cultivate your mysticism and ability to transcend the everyday. Alllow yourself to escape and to enter into projects that give a sense of connection to the greater whole. Develop your sense of identity in a holistic manner, feeding mind, body and spirit. Allow your life to flow in the cosmic sea. Pay close attention to your dreams for they will guide you.

Developing the qualities of your Sun-sign is a great step towards finding that inner sense of fulfilment that most of us are looking for yet cannot quite name. Yet there is another important placement as regards your astrological Sun. This is the house it is placed in. The house will be a number from one to twelve and should easily be obtainable from your astrological chart data. If you cannot see a number clearly look at the actual chart and count anti-clockwise from the nine o-clock position in the chart (the Ascendant). The first house below the Ascendant is number one, the second house number two and so on, right round to number twelve, which finds its place directly above the Ascendant line. The house of the Sun represents an area of life and shows where you should focus your creative and vocational energies in order to find inner fulfilment and connect with your true nature.

With the Sun in the 1st house, your task is to radiate your personality to others, to become a leader, the person who initiates and starts things off. You should approach life with your heart centre open for all to see, shining as an example of someone proud to be the person they are.

With the Sun in the 2nd house, fulfilment comes through concentrating on self-value and building up your inner and outer resources. Establishing yourself as a person who can rely on themselves only, particularly in financial matters, is very important. There is also a sense of needing to define yourself as someone able to take care of themselves. Develop your self-reliance and work on self-esteem. Be proud of all your achievements in this area.

With the Sun in the 3rd your fulfilment is connected with teaching and learning. You may develop by taking courses or learning to teach others. Improving your academic skills or writing a dairy could bring a strong sense of identity. Developing your communication skills will be important and help you to find a sense of authority and direction. Brothers and sisters could be an important influence on your life path. Attend to any issues that arise with them with care; they may be significant in your own destiny.

If you have the Sun in the 4th house an understanding of your inner life and how your identity relates to your roots and family is crucial. Your ability to shine here is bound up with the extent to which you can illuminate your inner world and is closely connected with family and domestic issues. Focusing on your home life and reflecting on your lineage may hold clues to your fulfilment.

With the Sun in the 5th house you were born for pure creative expression. Act, dance, sing, write, and express yourself in whatever you do. Allow yourself playtime and the cultivation of an identity that is naturally joyful. Stamp your unique expression on all that you do.

If your Sun falls in the 6th house you may find yourself through routine and ritual. Develop a regular pattern to your life that honours your own being. Shine in your efficiency and service to others. Develop your understanding and authority in the mind-body connection. Finding a specialism of some kind may also be highly fulfilling.

With the Sun in the 7th house your life path has to involve other people. You may literally give your identity away to others, especially significant males. It is therefore advisable to cultivate a vocation that allows you to engage with others on a one-to-one level in a professional manner, such as a counsellor or consultant. Working with a business partner may also help to forge your identity.

If your Sun is placed in the 8th house you will not find fulfilment by living a surface existence. Your path is to traverse deeper and darker realms. Allow yourself to explore the taboo, the occult, the hidden matter of life. Develop authority in these areas and your identity will shine through as you illuminate what others call the darkness, yet which they do not really understand.

With the Sun in the 9th house your fulfilment is bound up with finding a meaning by which to live by. Explore philosophies and religions to gain a sense of just where your position lies. Go beyond the circumstances of your youth, outwards into life, expanding all that you have known to date. Take opportunities to travel and see the world; this too will help you find your true nature.

If you were born with the Sun in the 10th house you were born to be out in the public eye. Having a career or public role is extremely important to your sense of fulfilment. It is no good staying at home with this placement. You need to be out there, doing something, advancing your status and career. You will shine and be an authority to others as a leader, provided you allow your true nature to develop.

With the Sun placed in the 11th house you find your identity as leader of a group. Your fulfilment is bound up with shining in the collective. Teaching or leading others will be highly fulfilling, as will engaging with social concerns and political issues. Develop your social nature and join groups and associations that appeal. Within these you will find a platform from which to shine.

If you were born with the Sun in the 12th house then your identity is somewhat of a paradox. On the one hand you will find yourself in solitude, by spending sufficient time alone, away from everyday life, just focused on being quiet and who you really are. On the other hand there is a need to develop a sense of being connected to all humanity. You may work behind the scenes or in charitable or altruistic avenues. Developing your spirituality is vital to your fulfilment.

Now that we have considered the Sun in both sign and house, it is time to try and combine these two placements. Remember that as an approximate rule we can say that the sign gives the qualities you should develop whilst the house suggests the area of life it is appropriate for you to focus on.

The following examples should enable you to combine your own Sun sign and house position.

Sun in Sagittarius in the 2ⁿᵈ House

Here fulfilment comes through finding freedom and meaning through resources. Building an income that sets you free to live your dreams or enables you to continue your quest for a philosophy to live by is essential to your well-being. Vocations that combine exploration, growth and which promote self-value and self-sufficiency are ideal.

Sun in Virgo in the 5ᵗʰ House

The heart centre in this case is one that is devoted to pure self-expression but in quite specific and practical forms. Fulfilment could come through specialised forms of creativity or through some craft or skill that can then be sold or put to practical use.

Sun in Capricorn in the 7ᵗʰ House

Here the individual expression and fulfilment comes through relating to others and in learning to be an equal in all relationships. Becoming a professional that engages in one-to-one contact is ideal here, as is the development of relationships that have a clear structure or committed form. A sense of vocation comes from mastering personal boundaries whilst still engaging with other people.

Sun in Aries in the 10ᵗʰ House

This is an extremely dynamic placement, indicating someone who will find fulfilment through being a pioneer for all to see.

They need public adventure and to start projects that allow them to be a warrior in the world. A career or *go-getting* role of some kind is essential for this adventurous individual, who is not shy to be on the public stage.

Sun in Gemini in the 12th House

This placement has a need to develop a spiritual perspective on life and to involve with others and the world of dreams and the unconscious. Making a study of dreams through rational analysis or through writing would be an excellent start to finding fulfilment with this placement.

The Sun in Relationship

When you are actively working at developing your astrological Sun placement you are on your path to fulfilment and an inner sense of radiance and happiness. This in itself puts you in an excellent position to attract a soul-mate who will serve you at the highest level and support you in your own journey.

If you do not develop your Sun there might be a danger of projecting it onto your partner, particularly if you are female. When this happens it is as though we give a part of ourselves away, asking our partner to live our life for us and give us meaning. This does not ultimately bring a lasting sense of peace and fulfilment and it is far better to work on your own development and life centre rather than expecting a partner to provide it for you.

When we shine from our heart centre, others sit up and take notice; we are radiant and alive with our own creativity (and remember that creativity is far wider in meaning than just the conventional creative arts). We are closer to becoming who we really are and our vibrations are therefore at a high level.

Whilst you are developing your inner sense of vocation and creativity you may believe that you are not really working on your goal of finding a soul-mate. But you would be quite wrong! Strengthening your own sense of happiness and alignment to your true nature is virtually the only thing you need to do to really attract someone perfect for you at this stage in your life. The astrological Sun is a very important part of this, as is the Moon, which we shall consider next.

CHAPTER 5

UNDERSTANDING YOUR EMOTIONAL NEEDS

I N ASTROLOGY THERE IS A planet that describes what we fundamentally need in order to feel right with the world, in order to feel that we are okay on a day to day level. This is the planet that rules our emotions and daily experience: the Moon.

The Moon is an extremely powerful image for humanity. She appears bright in the sky on a clear night, and appears as big as the Sun despite in reality being much smaller. The beautiful harmony of the universe however, and the divine taste for proportion, has ensured that the luminaries appear equal in size to the human observer. Whilst the Sun is four-hundred times further away, the Moon is four-hundred times smaller. What a beautiful design!

The Sun and Moon form two vital parts of the human psyche. They are our inner masculine and feminine, our purpose and instinct, our creativity and our sense of preservation. Whilst the Sun is orientated towards the day and all that is public and on show, the Moon is the private sphere, the past, our inner self and emotional life.

It is absolutely vital to honour the Moon as shown in your astrological chart. Without this, it will be very difficult to feel nourished and protected on a fundamental level. First read about your Moon sign here, then read up about its house placement and the suggested strategies for increasing your sense of daily wellbeing.

Moon in Aries

Here emotional satisfaction is bound up with being dynamic and pioneering, with being first, and the best. There is instinctive desire for competition and assertion. If you have Aries Moon and you feel that you are a shrinking violet, afraid to go out there and be yourself, not caring what others think, then something is wrong!

With the Moon in Aries you nurture yourself by competing, by starting things off, by living in quite a dynamic whirl in your home and private life. This is not a patient placement and you feel good when you are active and doing things. Excite yourself with your own adventures and quests, and ensure that you clearly assert your needs honestly and directly. You can be a forceful individual, but you need to be on some level—this is simply an honest expression of who you are.

In your home and domestic life be assertive, and take action when you feel energised to do so.

Moon in Taurus

The Moon in Taurus craves peace and stability above all things. This is a very tranquil placement for the Moon and you must ensure you make your domestic and personal surroundings as comfortable and beautiful as you can. Having enough quiet time and cultivating a sense of security through your resources is very important.

Save a little money each month, but treat yourself with the odd beautiful thing for your home or a sensuous meal out. This is a very physical Moon, and a massage or other touch-based therapy might be just what you need to feel good in your own skin again.

At home, create an atmosphere that is tranquil, aesthetically pleasing, and that feels safe and secure.

Moon in Gemini

For the Moon in Gemini mental stimulation is extremely important. This is often the placement of the voracious reader, talker, or both. To feel good on a day to day basis, ensure you expose yourself to sufficient new interests, perhaps through newspapers or books, through many conversations or courses of study.

The Moon in Gemini needs to express its feelings in words. Talk or write on a daily basis—keeping a diary might be especially rewarding with this placement, almost necessary. With the Moon in Gemini you may not know exactly what you feel until you say it or write it down. And often, once you verbalise an emotion, you realise that statement was just the opposite of what you actually feel!

At home, you must have plenty to stimulate your curious

mind. A library ticket or computer with an internet connection might be essential! You also require sufficient space to breathe and might need time alone in order to calm the constant chatter of your mind.

Moon in Cancer

Cancer is the natural sign of the Moon and so here we have someone who is strongly lunar in nature. Attention to the feelings and the imagination is particularly important, and moodiness can be an issue as feelings wax and wane like the Moon itself.

The Moon in Cancer is very security conscious but it is emotional security that it craves most; attending to your most intimate or familial relationships might be very rewarding as you like to feel secure bonds are intact at all times. You will also benefit from feeling financially secure.

You need to nurture something in your life, whether it is creating a cosy home or beautiful garden, or some projects that you do at work; your attitude to life is a nurturer, someone who tends things carefully and with great attention.

Make your home as comfortable and secure as you can; allow yourself emotional ebb and flow, and honour the changes in your feelings. Pay particular attention to the lunar cycle, as you may be very receptive to the monthly ritual of the New and Full Moons.

Moon in Leo

The greatest need of the Moon in Leo is to shine and to stand out in its environment. This is a very heart-centred, creative and playful placement. Be sure to spend sufficient time expressing yourself, through whatever creative medium you favour, and also spend much time in 'play'.

It is no shame to act in a childlike manner on occasion with this placement; you are instinctively joyful, sunny and perhaps sometimes naïve. Love, laugh and live joyfully. Being dramatic and showy is also very nourishing for you.

With the Moon in Leo you need to feel proud; let yourself live in luxurious style, at least to the extent that you can afford. The odd showy item may do you the world of good in psychological terms.

Make your home a place you are proud of, with things that truly express your individuality and creativity.

Moon in Virgo

The Moon in Virgo must live an ordered existence. Creating a nourishing routine for yourself, a daily ritual that includes all the things that make you feel good and taken care of, is essential to your well-being. Ensure you live a tidy and well-organised life; keep lists and have a planner or diary to ensure all your appointments are in order.

This placement has innate love of classification and knowledge that can be applied. Feed your intelligence by applying yourself to the subjects that interest you and then using that knowledge in your daily life.

For the Moon in Virgo, over-control of the environment can be an issue. By all means order your life with care and precision, but allow yourself to let go of the reins just a little so that you do not miss the natural flow of the universe.

Make your home a paradise of cleanliness and order. A minimalist style in the home may suit you, but the most important factor is that everything has its place, as determined by you.

Moon in Libra

The Moon in Libra requires harmony and balance. It enjoys people to relate to so that it may find its own response in relation to them and deliberate thereon. The Moon in Libra has a natural sense of justice and is very rational. It also has innate style and taste. With this placement spend time cultivating your own style and make sure your daily environment has many beautiful items within it, to satisfy your inner hunger for aesthetic pleasures.

Relationships are important to the Moon in Libra so here the instinct for a partner may be very strong. Try to avoid feeling you can't be complete without someone else; attempt to find balance within yourself and reconcile all opposites. You are both male and female, man and woman, ugly and beautiful, confident and insecure.

Make your home a beautiful, stylish place where you may entertain and court your wide circle of friends and connections.

Moon in Scorpio

With Moon in Scorpio your emotions run very deep. It is essential that you allow yourself to get involved with matters that touch right at the heart of human existence: birth, death, or perhaps taboo subjects that others are afraid to engage with.

This is a Moon with powerful sexual needs. It is also a Moon sign that requires intensity in relationships; finding a powerful emotional bond can be important to relationship happiness. There can be a strong tendency to possessiveness and jealousy and a powerful need to seek revenge if one feels wounded. Concentrate on honouring your own emotions, of finding the depth and truth of who you really are. Being serious and deeply connected to your feeling life will be particularly nurturing.

At home you wish to feel deeply engaged; ensure you surround yourself with objects that are emotionally important and which express your own profundity.

Moon in Sagittarius

The principal expression of the Moon in Sagittarius is a love of freedom and exploration. To feel right with yourself you must allow yourself plenty of variety and new adventures in life which allow you to expand your sense of who you are.

Time outdoors may be very nourishing to you, as there is something instinctual about your need for large, open spaces. Travel is very nurturing also, and making a few trips beyond the confines of whatever you are used to is the key to indulging your growth-orientated nature. It may also be highly fulfilling to consider different philosophies of life and varying spiritual and religious views.

At home you need a great deal of space! Even if you cannot afford a large home try to cultivate a sense of freedom and expanse in your living environment. Ensure your home contains objects that express the diversity of cultures and philosophies in the world.

Moon in Capricorn

The Moon in Capricorn produces instincts that are serious, responsible and often very mature. This is someone who must achieve and there is often natural business talent. A Moon in Capricorn will become very miserable if they have no goal to which to work towards or if they cannot express their innate ambition and instinct to climb to the top of whatever their interest is.

The instincts of the Moon in Capricorn are to look to the long-term. Making ten or twenty year plans could be quite fulfilling but be careful to build some flexibility into them; you do not wish to over-control life and avoid the rich and exciting possibilities that may be in store for you.

At home the Moon in Capricorn will require a sense of stability and security. Home may be a source of pride and an asset which helps to fuel emotional security and wellbeing. Create an environment that supports your love of tradition, quality and time.

Moon in Aquarius

Moon in Aquarius can be very reflective and detached as regards its own emotions. You require intellectual stimulation and involvement with groups and friends in order to feel well and happy. Becoming involved in progressive activities or political causes may also be beneficial to your emotional health.

Living from your ideals and from principles is very nurturing for you, as is approaching life with an open-minded attitude and compassion for all human beings. Being socially conscious you may enjoy getting involved in particular groups that really embody the things you feel strongly about.

In your domestic life and day to day existence you may find it hard to concentrate on mundane matters. You somehow wish to detach and rise above it all; give yourself time to do this whether this is through reading, group activities or other interests.

Moon in Pisces

With this Moon you are very sensitive and love to escape into a romantic fantasy world. You benefit from time spent indulging in fantasies, for example through computer games or watching films. You may also enjoy becoming absorbed in a fiction book, in music or poetry.

The Moon in Pisces needs to feel connected with the whole of life at a deep level. Meditation or some spiritual practice can be highly nourishing, as can anything that allows one to feel inspired. Artistic or creative pursuits may be very nurturing ways of expressing this longing for something almost divine.

At home cultivate a sense of the mystical and inspirational. Allow some fantasy and escapism to come into the design of your home, as this will be particularly nurturing to your soul.

The house placement of the Moon is also very important. This information should be easily extractable from your chart. Look for the crescent Moon symbol and see which area of the chart it falls into. The first section below the Ascendant on the left hand side is house one and the other houses follow round in anti-clockwise rotation.

Moon in the 1st house

This placement suggests emotional fulfilment is bound up with the sense of oneself as an active, autonomous person. To feel good, ensure you start something new on a regular basis, even just a little thing that reminds you of your own ability to act in the world. Your feelings will influence everything you do in life so being in tune with them is essential. You may start things off by gently sensing your way through, and checking in with your intuition regularly could be very valuable as you journey through life.

Moon in the 2nd house

Here, the Moon requires a sense of security. Taking great care of your finances and possessions will assist you in feeling emotionally satisfied, as will developing your self-esteem as much as possible. Certain possessions may become very emotionally important to you and give a strong sense of security. Earning an income and being able to stand on your own two feet helps you to feel nourished and nurtured. Ensuring you feel comfortable in your body is extremely important to your emotional happiness.

Moon in the 3rd House

With the Moon in the 3rd, emotional wellbeing comes through being stimulated on a mental level, and through having sufficient interests and connections in the day to day environment. Taking a course of study or making time each day to read or write in your diary can be very important for those with this Moon-sign. Communicating your feelings is essential and there might be strong ties to female siblings, aunts or other relatives. You are emotionally in tune with the local environment around you and taking the time to appreciate your surroundings could be most nourishing.

Moon in the 4th House

This is the placement of the homebody. You feel good when you are safely contained in a homely environment and you are very private. Taking good care to provide a nurturing living space for yourself is very important to your emotional wellbeing. There will likely be strong feelings around your family, father, roots or heritage and exploring these issues may be important for your happiness. It is essential that you have a private space in which to let your real feelings out; nurturing your inner life is also highly nourishing.

Moon in the 5th House

Here the individual has a need for play and creativity in daily life. If this is your Moon make sure some 'playtime' is factored into every day where you can express yourself naturally and joyfully. You may find it nurturing to spend time playing with babies and children as they spark your own natural sense of joy and love of life. Allow yourself to be creative—with music, dance, and writing; whatever feels good. It doesn't matter about the quality of what you produce. For you nurturing is about being playful and creative and you will nourish yourself the more you let yourself do those things that bring you pure joy, regardless of any practical use they may or may not have.

Moon in the 6th House

With the Moon in the 6th house you require ritual and routine to feel emotionally strong. Spend some time ensuring your daily routine feels satisfying and nourishing to you. Take particular care with your food intake and diet. You may enjoy daily exercise and a particular eating regime. Nurturing the connection between mind and body may bring great benefits to your general wellbeing as could the development of specific skills and talents.

Moon in the 7th House

Having the Moon in the 7th can suggest you become easily dependent on another person. Having close relationships with other people is essential for your emotional wellbeing. Take the pressure off romantic associations by building strong bonds with friends, relatives and children, particularly females. Ensuring you retain a connection to your own feelings and emotions may be very important, as otherwise you may find them mirrored all too often in those around you. Finding work that allows you to nurture others or being strongly involved with women on a one-to-one basis can be very nourishing to your soul.

Moon in the 8th House

With the Moon in the 8th you need to live life on a deep level. Feed your natural hunger for depth by investigating psychology or a subject which allows you to penetrate beneath the surface. Do not pretend your emotional life is more superficial than it actually is. Allow yourself indulgence in a little of the dark side in your daily existence, be it through a horror film, or an activity which allows you to feel deeply. Nourish yourself by feeding your instinct for all that is hidden. You may find it emotionally fulfilling to deal with matters that others find difficult; you have a natural affinity with life's great passages, birth and death, and increasing your understanding of these will nurture your own soul.

Moon in the 9th House

If you have the Moon in the 9th then your emotional wellbeing comes through broadening your life in as many ways as possible. Feed yourself by nurturing any interest in philosophical questions you have or by planning frequent trips abroad. Learning a language or surrounding yourself in daily life with people from many different cultures and faiths could be highly nourishing. Your daily food in an emotional sense revolves around reaching broader and higher than your current situation. It is essential you allow yourself to open to all that takes you beyond your current level of knowledge and understanding. Nurturing for you is ideas and experiences that give you broad vision and an appreciation of the vast principles overarching human existence.

Moon in the 10th House

With the Moon in the 10th your emotional wellbeing is bound up with your career and being out in the world. Nurture yourself by putting in enough time and energy so that you feel you are making progress in your life. Achievement and moving up in the eyes of the world are vital facets of nourishment with this placement. In daily life make goals and targets, for this is a nurturing activity for you. Embrace opportunities to be in the public eye; this is your natural place! Perhaps you enjoy performing on a stage or at work in front of many people. Leading others and becoming an authority may also be highly nourishing to your soul.

Moon in the 11th House

This placement suggests that emotional happiness may be found with friends or in collective situations. Make plenty of time in daily life for socialising or being part of groups or teams as this will increase your sense of wellbeing. You feel at home when amongst a number of like-minded people so clubs, associations and general social involvement is important to your sense of feeling nurtured. You will enjoy friendships, particularly with women, which are very nourishing and supportive.

Moon in the 12th House

With the Moon in the 12th you may feel nurtured by spending time alone away from the hubbub of daily life. To feel satisfied you need to connect with the divine on a daily level; and there is also a sense of natural escapism with this placement. Cultivating a daily meditation practice would be an ideal way to find nourishment. Your soul craves inspiration: music, poetry, and anything creative that enables you to find that all-important connection with something beyond yourself. You may also find nurturing through fantasy, films, video-games or role-play; those activities that enable you to lose yourself and become at one with another or some greater concept.

COMBINING THE MOON'S SIGN AND HOUSE

Combining the Moon's sign and house will give you a more integrated view of the Moon's placement in your chart. Remember that this shows what you need in daily life in order to feel emotionally happy. Its importance therefore cannot be emphasised too much. Some examples follow here so that you can put together your own combined interpretation.

MOON IN GEMINI IN THE 12TH HOUSE

There is a powerful need to communicate and express emotions here but also the need for solitude and connection with the divine. Writing in private might be a perfect outlet for this placement as could a mixture of communicating feelings but then retreating to spend time alone.

MOON IN SCORPIO IN THE 9TH HOUSE

Emotional intensity for expanded awareness is essential to this Moon placement. The individual would do well to engage deeply with their natural thirst for philosophical ideas and meaning. Finding a philosophy by which they can live intensely on a day to day level could be highly nurturing.

Moon in Aries in the 5th House

For this person, risk-taking and rushing out to try new creative ventures may be very emotionally fulfilling. Each day allow yourself time to play and be creative in a manner that allows you to be pioneering and adventurous.

Moon in Cancer in the 1st House

Your own emotional experience is very important to you. Allow time each day to just be with your feelings and allow them to guide you in what action to take. Be wary however of allowing your life to be dominated by your moods and sometimes negative feelings.

Moon in Libra in the 4th House

Balance, harmony and a pleasing home environment is very important to the emotional happiness of this individual. Developing considerate family relationships or finding a connection to one's roots and heritage through rational reflection and evaluation may be highly fulfilling. Decorating the home and bringing to it your own taste and style may be very important.

The Moon as Indicator of Mother

The Moon has another very important feature in an astrological chart, which is its symbolic association with mother and any female who plays a nurturing role. Our Moon-sign and house can therefore indicate something about how we perceived our own mother.

Because the Moon is so very important to our fundamental wellbeing and vital to relationship happiness, a poor relationship with our mother can impact us quite strongly when we try to connect with other people on an emotional level. If for some reason we are still struggling to relate to our mother or the person who was our early role-model as regards nurturing, we may struggle to nurture ourselves adequately in adult life.

In your journey to find a soul-mate therefore, taking some time out to contemplate any mother problems and do what we can to heal that relationship, if required, may be a very valuable exercise. You might like to start with the sign and house placement of your Moon to get a sense of how you may have perceived your mother when young. What you should always remember however, is that this is your subjective perception, and the mother in reality may have been quite different. We never really have a totally objective view of another person, just our own experience and perception. It is important therefore that we take responsibility for whatever was co-created between us, forgive any perceived hurts, and give ourselves permission to really care and support ourselves as adults.

If your Moon is in Scorpio in the 4th house for example you may have a view of your mother as someone very powerful and controlling; a woman who held the home under spell when you were young and ruled it with strength, power and perhaps on occasion a cruel or ruthless streak. Your mother may actually not have been like this, but your own energy pattern disposes you to seeing a mother figure that would have had a forceful presence in the home, and thus you are likely to have been more sensitive to any such qualities.

Using this image as a starting point you may like to try and see where you could have co-created any difficult experience you had with your mother. You have your energy pattern, and she has hers, and what occurred between you was the meeting of two souls. As the mother she can take greater responsibility for whatever occurred when you were a child, but that is not the case anymore. Try to take back any projection you may have had on her and recognise that you could have brought out some of the less desirable qualities of your Moon-sign in her, merely through who you were. This is not to attach any blame to you; it is simply to recognise that life is always a co-created journey of experience.

As an adult you are now able to see your mother in more realistic terms. If there is any issue with her remember that she may not have got the nurturing she required either; imagine her as a little girl also needing love and affection, just as you did. Now, in the present, is your capacity to seize any negativity around your mother. Seize it, and let it go. You are an adult now, and able to nurture yourself perfectly adequately.

As another example, suppose your Moon is in Aries in the 5th house. Perhaps you view your mother as very aggressive, selfish or forceful, a loud presence who was only concerned with her own self-expression. There may be some truth in this, and there may not be. But there is something in your soul that needed a passionate, bold, creative female in your early life. This is because this archetype wishes to express within you as an adult. Recognise your own part in whatever drama there was, release it, and move forward to emotional happiness by expressing your own natural dynamism and creativity.

With a soul-mate waiting for us, we cannot afford to hold on to negative emotions from the past, particularly around our mother!

We will return to the Moon in chapter twelve when we will reconsider it in the context of a relationship situation.

Chapter 6

Understanding Your Greatest Fears

The planet Saturn had a bad reputation in traditional astrology, being known as the greater malefic. His poor image was perhaps associated with the qualities he represents: hard lessons, responsibilities, duties, unrelenting justice of an eye-for-an-eye kind, and absolute commitment to reality of the most mundane variety.

These characteristics may not sound the most attractive, but they are absolutely necessary for a full and rewarding life here on Earth. Without Saturn our lives would not contain the necessary structure or organisation needed to get through everyday existence. Happily, Saturn has undergone a revision in modern astrology, and we now recognise him as an essential principle in our lives.

For example, Saturn is symbolic of our bones and skeleton, the very structure by which our body is held up. He also represents the limits of life. An awareness of our own mortality is essential to us finding a meaning to our lives, of feeling that what we do is important, because ultimately this particular life does not go on forever.

This chapter is called understanding your greatest fears and the reason for this is that Saturn often represents a place of fear within us, an area of life so important that we have great trepidation or insecurity around it. This fear can be seen as a key life challenge, one that needs to be tackled and grappled with.

Dealing with our greatest fears or challenges in life gives us the potential for mastery in that very area. And this is exactly what Saturn represents. Once initial fears have been overcome, we can work on our relationship with Saturn, striving to always improve and better our efforts. Our ultimate reward is the mastery and pinnacle of achievement that Saturn symbolises.

Saturn's metal is lead. The medieval alchemists attempted to turn lead into gold. This was symbolic of the psycho-spiritual process that occurs when we turn our own Saturn fears into the gold of pure personal expression. This is the joy that comes from spiritual discipline and mastery of a particular area of life.

This is one planet that cannot be worked on in a purely psychological manner. Saturn demands real achievement and real results. Often honouring this god will involve going out and doing something in the world; really getting that degree or qualification, making a substantial commitment in a relationship, or going for that public speaking engagement that seemed so impossible at one stage.

Working with your Saturn will bring you an immense sense of accomplishment. Facing our fears honestly and tackling them always brings rewards. Your ego will strengthen in a healthy manner, and this will increase the sense you have of yourself as an individual in the world. This can only aid your relationships, as you feel a more solid sense of who you really are.

Here we will examine Saturn by sign and house so that you can begin to find your own sense of where you may need to tackle his demands.

Saturn in Aries

Here there may be a basic fear of being assertive or dynamic. There is some issue around self-expression and going after what you want. Mastery of self-directed action is the goal and what you should strive for. Fears around autonomy or somehow being constrained in expressing your own desires may be apparent. If such fears can be worked with, a gift awaits. This gift is the mastery of personal boundaries, of being able to act with control and an appropriate use of boundaries, whilst fully expressing your own pioneering ability and initiative.

Saturn in Taurus

In this placement there may be fears around material and physical security. We may feel that we are always insecure, lacking in money, comfort or in basic physical essentials for living. We may also feel that we do not have a beautiful physical environment in which to live, that we lack an experience of the delights of nature. This is also a placement that could indicate getting quite stuck, and being unable to move forward through perceived limitations. There might be a fear of trying to build a secure future for ourselves; perhaps we believe that it might all be taken away or that we simply are not capable of creating the security we crave.

Working with any such fears brings the gift of mastery over the material world, and particularly in relation to the sense of security we feel. We may actually become very talented at building resources for ourselves, at securing property and possessions, and at building a solid and healthy bank account balance!

Saturn in Gemini

Here there may be fears around self-expression or intellectual attainment. You may feel that you cannot express yourself as freely as you would like to. Language or being unable to communicate may be powerful issues in your life. Early schooling may have been difficult or brought a very strict and authoritarian slant to learning which has resulted in a fearful approach to academic studies and a dislike of formal schooling.

Yet this placement suggests that communicative or educational achievement is very important to you. It is never too late to start studying something, and to complete it, or to improve your communication skills. Learning a language and attaining a level of mastery in doing so might be particularly fulfilling. Saturn in Gemini actually has the potential to be a brilliant scholar or wit, and initial limitations in this area, with a bit of hard mental effort, can be turned to magnificent achievements.

Saturn in Cancer

Fears around emotional security and family matters may dominate with Saturn in Cancer. One's fears come out in close, domestic situations, perhaps through family commitments or responsibilities. There may also be a fear around emotional expression and a sense of being limited in how one can really express what one is feeling. There may be a sense of lack around nurturing, as though one was never really nurtured on the feeling level. Another possibility is fears around imaginative expression.

The gift of Saturn in Cancer is to learn a true structuring of the emotions and to take on any necessary duties or responsibilities that revolve around home, mother or family and see them as a learning experience for soul-growth. Saturn in Cancer can ultimately become a very strong and supportive figure in the family environment. It can learn that true nurturing can also involve some boundaries and become a strong figure able to provide a sense of safety and emotional support to others.

Saturn in Leo

Saturn in Leo can never be loved enough. You may feel as though you are never really noticed or are ignored and unloved even when that is not the case. There may also be a sense of not being special or important enough. Blocks on creativity and dramatic self-expression may also be a possibility.

The gift of Saturn in Leo is to overcome any feelings of not being important, recognised or special by making the effort to develop your own creativity and authority. Allow yourself to shine as someone of authority and leadership and overcome fears of putting yourself forward and into the limelight. In this way you will experience the gold of Saturn.

Saturn in Virgo

With Saturn in Virgo there may be fears around routines and rituals and around one's own capacity to put knowledge to use.

Work and specific expression of skills may be an area that seems somehow frightening or difficult and one may experience many duties or tasks around work, diet or health. Any such fears can sometimes result in an over-compensation effect, so that the Saturn in Virgo individual is extremely exacting and critical, always trying to perfect the people and situations around him or her. This can lead to a high degree of nervous tension.

The gift of Saturn in Virgo is that ultimately it is a brilliant and insightful critic of the highest order. It has the potential to master some specific skill, perhaps connected to the mind/body link or the use of a specialised area of knowledge. This will come if the Saturn in Virgo individual can translate their initial fears into hard work, channelling their energy into a particular aspect of life so that they then become an expert, with full rights to critique and try to perfect others!

Saturn in Libra

With Saturn in Libra our fears may revolve around keeping the peace or having to over-compromise. We may shy away from diplomacy or engagement with others, fearing that we will lose our boundaries and be unable to retain our identity. We may have an active dislike of justice and fairness, seeing these concepts as eroding the freedoms of the individual for example.

Saturn is strong in Libra, and it may not therefore take too much effort to make the best of this placement. With some effort at understanding there are two sides to every story, the Saturn in Libra individual may become an excellent arbiter or judge, being totally fair and just. This is someone able to find the perfect balance and to take responsibilities upon themselves with a sense of grace.

Saturn in Scorpio

With Saturn in Scorpio we may fear the dark, anything that is deep and hidden. Powerful emotions may scare us and we may be disinclined to look too deeply at a situation because we do not want to see the motives lying under the surface. Our own darkness could frighten us with Saturn in Scorpio. Any such fears can result in an individual that may lash out quite viciously if its buttons are pressed, and who may show great suspicion and paranoia over matters which in reality are sources of fear.

The gift of Saturn in Scorpio is the attainment of mastery as regards a realistic appreciation of life's darker and deeper side. The Saturn in Scorpio individual has the ability to appreciate the reality of crisis and tragedy, and to understand that dark events play out in life and cannot be avoided altogether.

Saturn in Sagittarius

Saturn in Sagittarius may have fears around seeing the bigger picture or moving out into wider experiences of life. We may fear venturing out of our familiar circumstances or level of understanding and knowledge, not wishing to open to the possibilities of 'higher' ideas. This placement might also suggest a fear of growth; we may prefer to stay just as we are. Additionally there might also be a fear of God or of religion, and we may see others as being very dogmatic and take that as evidence that all beliefs are to be strongly questioned.

The gift of Saturn in Sagittarius is to find a sense of mastery and achievement in expanding one's horizons. Moving away from where one currently is to new, broader vistas of experience may ultimately become one's great strength with his placement. Fear of the unknown and of the future is replaced by ability to deal with these areas with ease and confidence.

Saturn in Capricorn

With Saturn in Capricorn there could be a fear of achievement, of having status or being seen as someone conventional. Responsibilities and duties may be initially dreaded and strongly resisted. We may not want to admit our own ambitions with this placement, believing ourselves to be above such matters. Secret materialism may also be an issue, as we resist conceiving of ourselves as people to whom money and material possessions are important.

The gift of Saturn in Capricorn is the gift of achievement of worldly ambitions. This is a superb placement to attain mastery in business or in going after our goals, of climbing right to the top of the mountain. With Saturn in Capricorn we will have to work every step up with great effort, but we have an excellent chance of succeeding.

Saturn in Aquarius

Saturn in Aquarius may have fears around being part of the collective pool of humanity, and be uneasy about progressive or technological advancement. There may be a sense of being over-detached and there could be a fear around rational thinking, lest it take one to places one does not want to go. There might also be a dread or resistance to living from a set of principles and forever refraining from putting them into practice.

The gift of Saturn in Aquarius is of the ability for great reflection. This is the detached thinker par excellence. A person of great principle and high-mindedness may be found with this placement, once any initial fears have been overcome.

Saturn in Pisces

With Saturn in Pisces there could be fears of letting go, of being in the flow of life. It may seem as if chaos may rush in the minute control is loosened. We may distrust and fear our intuition or our dreams and have a sense that life is constantly on the edge of dissolution. As we build up structures in our lives, they may suddenly crumble beneath our feet, drifting away to nothing. This may give us a great fear of trying to do anything about the seeming chaos we find ourselves in.

The gift of Saturn in Pisces is the ability to manifest that which is intangible. We may be able to make something real and concrete from our visions and dreams or to find achievement through music, art or poetry.

The sign placement of Saturn will be the same for many people born within a year or two of each other. Although it is important, it is not therefore as important on a personal level as the actual house placement of Saturn. Thus the lessons of the house where your Saturn is may take priority in terms of considering where to focus your conscious efforts for development. There is some overlap between the sign and house placements. For example, Saturn in the 1st house may have some of the issues of Saturn in Aries. They are not however totally synonymous, and we will therefore consider each house placement in turn.

Saturn in the 1st House

With Saturn in the 1st house there may be difficulties around asserting the self. This denotes a very serious individual, who may often come across to others as very controlled, even cold. There may be fears around starting new ventures and a sense of being limited in one's identity and approach to life. Shyness and reserve might be particular problems when we are young.

The gift of Saturn in the 1st is that of a solid and secure personality, a person of maturity, seriousness and realism. This is the true pragmatist, and the individual who can meet life with a sense of what it is really all about. When initial fears about expressing the self and being who one is have been faced, we have a strong and stable individual, who may have a talent for dealing pragmatically with all that life throws at them.

Saturn in the 2nd House

With Saturn in the 2nd there may be fears around self-value and self-esteem. There is a sense of lack that could translate to financial lack, causing a keen sense that there is never enough to go round or that one must struggle to survive in this world. The 2nd house Saturn individual may feel that life is a struggle and that there are constant limitations to achieving material security.

The gift of Saturn in the 2nd is the ability to master one's own finances. Cultivating a strong sense of self-worth and self-value is the deeper layer to this, and when this is achieved, one may find natural attention is paid to the bank balance and proper valuing of one's talents.

Saturn in the 3rd House

With Saturn in the 3rd there may be fears or difficulties around communication and intellectual ability. We may feel we simply are not smart enough and that we cannot express ourselves or ask for our needs to be met. Brothers or sisters may also seem to be a limiting factor in our life, inhibiting our ability to really be ourselves. They may be a burden in some manner, and require us to adopt an attitude of responsibility towards them.

The gift of Saturn in the 3rd house is that of attaining mastery in study, learning and communication. We may find it very rewarding to take a course of study and stick with it right to the end, so that we achieve the public acknowledgement of having attained something for our efforts. Making an effort to be very clear in our communications may also be highly fulfilling and ultimately we may be able to teach others to express themselves with clarity and purpose.

Saturn in the 4th House

With Saturn in the 4th there may be fears around home and family. Perhaps we feel that we do not belong anywhere, and have no roots or firm foundation from which to go out into the world. The father may be seen as a particular source of limitation and our background may be seen as a somewhat cold affair, perhaps not having provided us with a real sense of comfort or nurturing.

The gift of Saturn in the 4th is to attain a sense of mastery over the home life and inner emotional sphere. Perhaps we enjoy order and structure in our home or even start a business connected to property. We may also be able to cultivate an ability to structure our inner lives and understand our own fears or limitations. Ultimately we may build-up such a strong sense of inner security that this acts as a very firm foundation from which we can go out and meet life.

Saturn in the 5th House

With Saturn in the 5th house we may fear expressing ourselves and believe that we have no creative talents. Our 'playtime' may somehow always seem to morph into more work, responsibilities or limitations. We may also have fears around having children or fully allowing ourselves to enjoy our free-time.

The gift of Saturn here is the ability to turn creative and recreational expression into something very serious and tangible. We may be able to form a business or career out of the things we do for the pure joy of them, and to structure our free-time to make the very best use of it. We may ultimately find joy in the responsibility that parenthood brings and a strong sense of satisfaction at our own creative efforts.

Saturn in the 6th House

With Saturn in the 6th house fears or difficulties may arise in issues of daily routine and work. We may hate the idea of getting into a rut, becoming part of the rat race, stuck in the same old 'groundhog' day. There may also be dissociation between the mind and body connection and physical limitations may seem part of our daily lot.

The gift of this placement lies in understanding that ritual and routine is actually a crucial component to our psychological happiness. Having responsibilities in daily life and work, and a sense of order and structure, may ultimately be highly fulfilling. With any initial fears overcome, we may willingly embrace our role as a reliable and practical figure in daily life. Ultimately our lives may become brilliant examples of sound day to day management and organisation.

Saturn in the 7th House

Saturn in the 7th house may indicate fears around relationships. Perhaps we do not really want to reveal ourselves to another or have a block on commitment. Being involved with someone else can be a strong source of anxiety with this placement, and the result may be that we sabotage our own relationships, perhaps through being too stern or serious, or rejecting those who ask for commitment and loyalty.

The gift of Saturn in the 7th is the ability to create a long-term stable partnership that is serious and mature. We may particularly excel in having a business partner or colleague with whom we work closely in a professional situation. Our path to inner treasure lies in the strength and responsibility that will ultimately characterise our partnerships.

Saturn in the 8th House

With Saturn in the 8th house there can be a fear around true sharing of the self. Intimacy with another may be avoided, as we do not really trust other people enough to get very close to them. We may also have a dread of what is under the surface of life, of deep emotions and of hidden matters. We could find ourselves steering clear of taboo subjects or of those which look beneath the surface, like psychology and astrology.

The gift of this placement is that ultimately we can come to master the realm of the hidden and shared exchange. We may be able to create relationships that appropriately maintain our own boundaries. Further, we may develop a structured exploration of hidden matters, carefully peeking beneath the surface to consider that what may be found lurking is not so scary after all.

Saturn in the 9th House

With Saturn in the 9th house there may be fears around higher beliefs. Religion may seem an oppressive and heavy force, with a stern and harsh God judging all that we do. We may struggle to find a meaning in life and avoid thinking about spiritual or philosophical questions. There may also be resistance to expanding our lives through travel. Even if we do go abroad we may remain impervious to what we might learn from opening up to other cultures, preferring to remain with the tried and tested of our own present understanding.

The gift of Saturn in the 9th is to come to a very serious and mature understanding of our own religious or spiritual worldview (which might of course be atheism). With hard thought and the benefit of experience we are able to find a philosophy of life by which to live. If God plays a role in that belief we may come to see him as a harsh but wise teacher, rather than simply punitive and judgemental. We may also develop an ability to realistically appraise other cultures from our own.

Saturn in the 10th house

With Saturn in the 10th house there may be fears around pursuing a career or public success. We may be held back by a sense that we will not be good enough, or that others will laugh or make fun of us if we aim too highly or have ambitions above our station. Our mother may be seen as a strongly authoritarian figure who perhaps limits us in our career choice or who has an overly controlling influence.

The gift of Saturn in the 10th is to genuinely achieve something publicly. The career is very important and working towards long-term goals and ambitions as regards one's own status and career advancement is essential. With this placement it is possible to rise to the top of one's career, although it will likely be hard-won, with step by step progress making the end result very solid and sound.

Saturn in the 11th House

With Saturn in the 11th there may be a fear around group situations. We may feel uncomfortable and odd when we are amongst others, and feel that we do not really have many friends with whom to associate. As a result we may shy away from joining groups or courses, believing that we are unlikely to fit in and are better off alone.

The gift of Saturn in the 11th is ultimately to find the courage to join in with others, and we may be surprised when we make the effort. We may become an authority within a group, a leader who is respected and admired. With some work it is likely we can also find long-lasting friendships that stand the test of time.

Saturn in the 12th House

With Saturn in the 12th there may be fears around being isolated. Loneliness could be our greatest concern. We may fear that when alone we will dissolve and disappear and find it hard to have a strong sense of self or who we are. There may also be fears around dreams or letting go, a sense that we are not quite safe in the world of sleep or that something is lurking just outside of our normal, waking viewpoint.

The gift of Saturn in the 12th may be that in solitude and contemplation we actually find a very solid sense of self waiting for us, just where we least expect it. This placement has a hermit or monkish quality, and in meditation we may find the gifts of a strong and serious nature, just waiting to be uncovered.

Once we have an understanding of our Saturn by sign and house we can try to combine the information to build up a fuller picture. The following examples may help you to do this.

Saturn in Leo in the 3rd House

Here recognition for one's intellectual achievements is essential. We may fear we are not good enough until we have collected many qualifications that increase our status. Communication may also be vital to us, and expressing ourselves from the heart is a key challenge. Ultimately we may find that we become an authority in the area of self-expression or attain academic honours that give us a sense of our own uniqueness and special abilities.

Saturn in Gemini in the 12th House

Here we may fear being isolated and alone, unable to communicate with others and express our ideas. Taking the time to diarise or write in private might be a way out of this feeling of alienation. A course of spiritual study might also be highly satisfying and help us achieve a sense of mastery. We may actually find that we can achieve great things in private, for example writing our masterpiece or engaging in some heavy-duty study.

Saturn in Cancer in the 2nd House

With this Saturn we may feel that we are lacking in material resources, that we are not good enough to have nice things for ourselves. This may be particularly harsh on an emotional level—perhaps we feel we cannot provide enough for our family or those who depend on us. Rationally appraising our situation and nurturing our own efforts to improve our resources will help us achieve inner stability. When we have attained a sufficient sense of self-worth, such that we feel empowered to honour our own emotions, it is likely we may be able to achieve a stable and well-managed financial situation.

Saturn in Libra in the 11th House

With Saturn in Libra in the 11th house we may feel awkward and uncomfortable in group situations, perhaps experiencing our autonomy being compromised in some way. We may be too obliging and somehow forget to assert our own needs when around others, thereby ending up with feelings of frustration and not really belonging. If we can learn to balance our sense of justice to include that which is fair to ourselves, we may become a respected member of a group, able to arbitrate and act diplomatically, thereby bringing a greater sense of harmony and stability.

Wherever your Saturn is placed, it is likely that some conscious effort will be needed in order that you contact him completely, and ensure you have a healthy relationship to the area of life he represents for you. Going out and trying to achieve something tangible in the area of life Saturn indicates is often a very good strategy, for Saturn is a planet of this world, and often cannot be dealt with purely on a psychological level. Overcoming an inner fear involves recognising and understanding it, but then doing something about it!

Important Saturn Ages

You may be able to get in touch with your Saturn in particular at key ages that represent important movements by him to your birth chart. These ages are approximately the same for everyone and are 29-30 and 57-59 in particular. These ages represent 'reckonings', when you are asked to evaluate where you have got to in your life so far, and how well you are doing in terms of turning your fears into strengths. If you have been operating primarily from fear and insecurity until now, you are likely to face a crisis. This crisis however is the outward face of opportunity, when you have a chance to turn your life around and make it a more authentic expression of who you really are. You can therefore use these important ages to address the question of whether you have really faced your fears and gone after those things that are ultimately so important to you and your happiness.

Other important Saturn ages are 36-37, 43-44, and 50-51. These are mini staging points for the more important Saturn ages discussed above. But events and processes at these times may have similar themes, and recall the issues from the previous seven-year point. Saturn always asks us to be realistic, to face the truth of our lives and choices, and to become more authentic and in touch with our true ambitions.

CHAPTER 7

YOUR KEY DEVELOPMENTAL PATH

THE NORTH AND SOUTH NODES of the Moon represent the intersection of the orbital planes of both the Sun and the Moon. They are thus a combination of the two most fundamental portions of our nature, our heart centre (Sun) and our instinctual self (Moon). We can see them as a blend of our inner male and female, of the two most important energies within us. They are like an inner mystical marriage that brings together the essential elements of our nature into two points, one representing the route we are coming from, and the other the route we need to move towards.

The nodes are associated with destiny, and the conscious development of the North Node end in particular is often highly important. The nodes are also often associated with important people coming into our lives. We can therefore see them as indicative of key relationships and individuals who will spur us on to our own highest path.

It should be a straightforward matter to read off the sign and house position of your Moon's North Node. The South Node will always be placed exactly opposite the North, and therefore takes the opposite sign and house. For example, if your North Node is in Cancer in the 11th house, then your South Node is in Capricorn in the 5th house.

In terms of basic meaning, we can see the North Node as representing what we should strive to move towards whilst the South Node represents what we already have, and can to an extent leave behind. We should not however adopt a simplistic notion of 'North Node good' and 'South Node bad'. Ultimately we should strive for balance in living each end of the axis. However, because the South Node represents what we can already do well to some extent we do need to make a conscious shift to the North Node before we can move back to a place of greater balance.

We will consider the nodal axis firstly in the signs, and then in the houses.

North Node in Aries, South Node in Libra

Here your task is to move towards greater action, independence and autonomy using your natural diplomatic skills. It may be too tempting to fall back into compromise or consideration of the needs of others, thereby neglecting your own need to develop assertiveness and forceful expression of who you really are. Your innate talents are diplomacy, and a strong sense of fairness and justice. But you may lack initiative and the courage to go after things on your own, to really pursue your own adventures and wants regardless of what anybody else thinks. Taking a leap into the unknown, into something that is totally for you, about you or is a passionate expression of your desires, may be highly fulfilling.

North Node in Taurus, South Node in Scorpio

Here your task is to move towards a life of simplicity and security, by using your natural intensity and analytical ability. You may be naturally suspicious and secretive, and good at seeing beneath the surface of life, penetrating through to the deeper layers. What lies beneath may be a constant fascination, but could hold you back. Moving consciously towards simple and natural pleasures is highly beneficial to your soul. Appreciating the beauty of the physical body and natural environment for example can really expand your experiences and open up a new world.

North Node in Gemini, South Node in Sagittarius

Here you should move towards curiosity and interest in daily life and appreciate logical and rational enquiry, pursuing this whilst using your innate ability to see the bigger picture. It may be all too easy for you to fall back into generalisations or broad beliefs about things that do not really stand up to scrutiny when they are logically analysed and tested. Experimenting with subjecting your beliefs to rigorous testing and logical questioning could be very beneficial. You may also have a tendency to lecture on great themes or topics which span vast subject areas. Allowing yourself enjoyment of the beauty of a little precise knowledge about many different things, without trying to weave them altogether at first, may be very fulfilling.

North Node in Cancer, South Node in Capricorn

With this placement your task is to move towards qualities

of nurturing, imagination and sensitivity, using your innate pragmatism and realism as a driving force. You may find that you are innately ambitious and conscious of the rational reasons why certain courses of action will benefit you most. Yet sticking with what is sensible and makes rational and practical sense will be unlikely to help you move forward. Embracing a more intuitive or imaginative way of relating to life may be highly fulfilling. Following your feelings and the ebb and flow of emotions may help you to move into new directions, within which you will then be able to use your natural pragmatism and common-sense.

North Node in Leo, South Node in Aquarius

Here your task is to move towards honouring your own creative and unique gifts whilst using your natural concern for collective principles and wider humanitarian concerns. It is all too easy for you to get lost in the concerns of others, to be a friend to all and to be open-minded, tolerant and compassionate. But your own self-expression could get lost in this. Making an effort to express yourself with confidence and a powerful sense of uniqueness will be highly beneficial. Allowing your own creativity to shine through, rather than just being one amongst many, is an important part of your soul task in this lifetime.

North Node in Virgo, South Node in Pisces.

Here your task is to move towards refining a particular skill using your natural intuition and holistic vision. It is all too easy for you to escape into fantasy or get lost in clouds of imagination or artistic expression. Chaos and a lack of boundaries may be familiar friends and you may be very fluid and able to meander through life with great openness and sensitivity. Yet these traits could hold you back if you do not move towards a greater sense of discrimination and pragmatic analysis in day to day life. Refining your skills and developing specialist knowledge will be very beneficial, as will forcing yourself to engage with the details and practical requirements of daily life.

North Node in Libra, South Node in Aries

Here your task is to cultivate harmony and diplomacy in your relationships, using your innate courage, passion and assertion to do so. Independence, autonomy and self-directed action come very easily to you. You love to be alone to pursue adventures and to conquer some new area of experience. Yet this great sense of self and independence could hold you back. Your soul asks you to learn greater cooperation and engagement with others. Entering into relationships and learning about compromise will be very beneficial to you, and ultimately allow you to lead and direct with greater understanding of other people.

North Node in Scorpio, South Node in Taurus

Here your task is to cultivate depth and intensity using your natural peace and tranquillity. Enjoyment of the senses and of the good things in life comes very easily to you. You are a beacon of stability and tranquillity, and enjoy security. You may enjoy a life where little is disrupted and your peace is undisturbed. Yet your soul requires you to go deeper. Consciously cultivating knowledge of what is beneath the surface, of hidden motivations and deeper and darker matters, is highly fulfilling to you. Transformations and crises may be blessings in disguise as they force you to grow and change through an appreciation of the important passages in life. Ultimately your natural stability will act as a rock from which you can understand the deeper side of life.

North Node in Sagittarius, South Node in Gemini

Here your task is to expand your worldview and broader picture of life using your natural inquisitiveness and rationality. It is all too easy for you to flit around here and there, gathering bits and pieces of information to logically analyse, but not attempting to bring them into some wider scheme of belief. Consciously moving towards finding meaning and a broad scheme by which to live is likely to be highly beneficial to your soul-growth. Your youthful inquisitiveness will ultimately serve you well in a healthy questioning of any broader system you adopt.

North Node in Capricorn, South Node in Cancer

Here your task is to develop long-range goals that are pragmatic and realistic using your innate imagination and ability to honour your feelings. You may be naturally inclined to focus on your own emotions and to fall back into subjective viewpoints or sulks that have no room for a more detached or pragmatic analysis. It is your soul's task to move towards an appreciation of what can come through sticking with something for the long-term, even when it does not feel good. Cultivating an understanding that mastery requires staying in there, regardless of temporary feelings of discontent, will be highly beneficial. Ultimately your natural sense of feeling will serve you well in allowing for movement within a long-term structure.

North Node in Aquarius, South Node in Leo

Here your task is to develop concern for humanity as a whole and find ideals to live by, using your innate creativity and self-expression to do so. You may be naturally concerned with your own creativity, with being unique and special, and with being the centre of some drama or other on a regular basis. You could be held back by this tendency however. Your soul requires you to move toward an appreciation of those around you, of humanity in general, and of the importance of the group. Friendships and social involvements may be one means through which you are able to find this wider understanding. Ultimately your natural expression and love of drama will enable you to enliven and invigorate any group to which you belong.

North Node in Pisces, South Node in Virgo

Here your task is to develop a connection to the whole of life using your innate focus and analytical abilities. Your natural inclination may be to analyse, discriminate and dissect information, easily applying that which is useful to you and discarding the rest. This could however hold you back, not allowing you to move forward to a place in which you can receive inspiration and connect to a greater sense of something beyond this existence. Allowing yourself to ease off any over-controlling instincts to a place where you can flow with the mysteries of life will be highly fulfilling for your soul, as will indulging in a little escapism; for example, through films, music, or drama. Ultimately your critical and analytical gifts will help you make the most of any inspiration you find.

Whilst the sign placement describes what qualities we must ultimately learn to balance, the house placement of the Nodes can suggest critical areas of life to our development. Often these life areas are ones that are of crucial relevance to the most important decisions of our lives. When you have a critical decision to make it is always worth bearing in mind the house and sign placement of your North Node and asking yourself whether it would be well-served by each of the options available to you. Whilst this should not be the only factor in any major decision it will give you food for thought as you reflect upon what course of action is likely to bring the most growth to you on your life's journey.

The house placement of the nodes

North Node in the First House, South Node in the Seventh House

With this placement, partners or other people may pull us back into regressive patterns of behaviour. We may need to make a strong, conscious effort to remember our own identity, and who we are, and express this with some force. Concentrating on what we need, rather than allowing ourselves to be drawn into the dramas of others may be an important element of our soul growth.

North Node in the Second House, South Node in the Eight House

With this placement, we may find ourselves financially dependent on other people or involved with them to the degree that we do not feel confident about our ability to live from our own resources. Putting effort into self-value and striving to build up security from our own resources and money can be very fulfilling with this placement, and necessary for our soul's path in this life.

North Node in the Third House, South Node in the Ninth House

Religious beliefs or overall concepts that have not been sufficiently analysed could be troublesome with this nodal axis; move towards greater analysis and intellectual treatment of your ideas, particularly those that have been inherited from the wider family. Our task here is to greater understanding of the local environment and our everyday communications; it may be tempting for us to look far and wide for answers but we may find that it is much closer to home that our path really lies.

North Node in the Fourth House, South Node in the Tenth House

With this placement, career and issues of status or public acclaim may pull us back into past patterns of behaviour that are not helpful to our growth. It may be easy for us to find success and honours, but this is not what our soul craves. Instead, there is a need to move towards honouring the home, family and inner life. We may need to look to our roots and past to find a sense of where we need to go in life and to tune in to our feelings and moods. Whilst we should not neglect our career, we may at critical times have to choose in favour of home, family and the inner life.

North Node in the 5th House, South Node in the 11th House

With the South Node in the 11th house, we may be constantly pulled back into social activities and friendships that leave us little room for exploring our own personal sense of creativity. Whilst we are talented in dealing with others and in social situations, conscious effort towards personal expression and doing things purely from one's own sense of creative joy may be important for soul growth. Learning to express oneself with no regard for what others may think could be a liberating and exhilarating experience.

North Node in the Sixth House, South Node in the Twelfth House

With this placement we may be tempted to fall back into escapism, into a private world that consists of our own fantasies and dreams, and bears little relation to the demands of daily existence. We love swimming in the vast waters of the collective unconscious, losing ourselves in meditation or in fantasy games or programmes. This tendency can however hold us back and our soul requires that we consciously strive towards understanding the demands of daily incarnation. Developing a specific routine in the day or holding down a regular job can be important experiences for this placement. Ultimately we will be able to bring our rich fantasy life into our day to day life, imbuing it with meaning and purpose.

North Node in the 7th House, South Node in the 1st House

With the South Node in the 1st house, our tendency may be to fall back on our own identity and operate from a feeling of being separate from others, putting our own view of life above all other things. Such independence could hold us back however, for our soul growth is served here by entering into partnerships, into relationships that allow us to fully appreciate another person. Critical life decisions may revolve around entering or staying in a partnership rather than choosing to go it alone. It will generally be the best course of action, in terms of soul-growth, to honour the partnership. Ultimately your own solid sense of identity will serve you well in relating to another person from a strong position.

North Node in the 8th House, South Node in the 2nd House

With this placement greater emphasis on sharing with another is required. Financial, emotional and sexual exchange are all areas that await exploration and which might be neglected as your tendency is to fall back on your own resources, without reference to another. Greater intimacy is what you should seek for your soul to grow, and it also aids you to look beneath the surface of life and explore what is hidden. Psychology, esoteric practices or taboo areas may be worthy of your attention, and you might need to move away from a too literal or material focus in life, in order to make the most of your gifts.

North Node in the 9th House, South Node in the 3rd House

With this placement growth comes through moving out into the wider world, taking opportunities to travel and experience cultures different from your own. Exploring theories on the meaning of life and religious beliefs can be very valuable, rather than falling back onto the opinions that surrounded you when you were growing up or which stem from rational analysis only. Your natural tendency here may be to take comfort in the local environment or in study that does not really stretch your mind or ask you to take a higher viewpoint. But your soul requires expansion, and a move beyond the confines of everyday knowledge. Ultimately your natural communicative gifts will serve you well as you move beyond the boundaries of your current experience.

North Node in the 10th House, South Node in the 4th house

With the South Node in the 4th house, you may feel inclined to focus your attention on home, family and roots. Your inner life and your private sphere may be all important and you may be very good at cultivating a strong basis from which to go out into life. It is likely however that you may have neglected your career or overt matters of status. Your soul requires that you reach up into some more public domain, that you have goals and ambitions, and that you make a place for yourself in the world. Ultimately the strong inner foundation you have created will serve you well as you explore a more public realm.

North Node in the 11th house, South Node in the 5th house

With this placement there is a natural tendency to fall back onto one's own joyful expression and individual creativity, without thinking about collective joy or the expression that could be found within a group or society. Your soul requires that you engage with other people, that you join groups or find an interest in other people that allows you to experience your identity as one of many rather than by yourself. Solidarity and friendship may be important learning experiences for you, and highly fulfilling. Ultimately your own creative streak will serve you well in your collective ventures.

North Node in the 12th House, South Node in the 6th House

With the South Node in the 6th much of your natural energy may fall towards the daily grind, with your working or health routine, and with dealing with the day to day affairs of material life. Such a focus can hold you back and your soul demands that you look beyond daily life to a vast, mystical realm where we are all connected and ultimately all become one. Exploring meditation or spiritual practices may help your soul find what it longs for, as could allowing your spirit to soar into artistic or inspirational realms. Escaping from the busyness of the everyday could be highly fulfilling for you, as could allowing more flow and magic to enter your experience. Ultimately your grip on mundane reality will serve you well as you navigate more mysterious waters.

Once we understand our nodal axis by sign and house it is time to try and integrate these two placements. The following examples should aid you in doing this for your own chart.

North Node in Libra in the 4th House, South Node in Aries in the 10th

Here the natural gifts are connected with independence and leadership in the public sphere. It may be instinctive for this person to climb the career ladder, firmly focused on exactly where they need to be. Yet true growth will come if they take the time to look within, to take others into account and to focus on their personal and family relationships. There is a need to find one's roots and inner life, before the real achievement of the 10th house can be manifested.

North Node in Capricorn in the 7th House, South Node in Cancer in the 1st

Here there is a natural tendency to depend on oneself, to be caught up in one's own subjective perception of the world and perhaps not all that interested in the work involved in creating a successful partnership. The key developmental task is to make the effort to have a real relationship with someone, one that is serious and for the long-term. This will ultimately increase the sense of emotional identity the individual has. Staying with a partnership for the long-term, even when one's own emotions do not accord, may be important to ultimate growth of the soul.

North Node in Taurus in the 6th House, South Node in Scorpio in the 12th

With this placement there can be a tendency to escape into a fantasy world, with dark desires and perhaps sexual fantasies playing a primary role. Development comes through taking a simpler approach to daily life and the world, through real physical experiences of touch and of working in a routine but tangible manner. This will eventually aid the rich fantasy life that comes so naturally. A regular, wholesome job or daily routine that honours simple pleasures may be welcome relief from the intensity of the fantasy world that comes so naturally.

Working with our nodal axis, with an awareness of what we need to move towards, and what comes naturally, is a crucial component in our self-development. It may be a lifetime's task to fully balance this axis, but it is well worth the effort.

We have now compiled all the information we need to assemble our True Self profile, which we will do in the next chapter.

Chapter 8

Assembling Your Unique True Self Profile

Now we have outlined the major factors involved in your personal horoscope, we can try and put all the information together.

Remember that we have discussed the following components:

- » The Ascendant—this shows how you approach life and says something about your journey in the world
- » The Sun—this is your heart centre, what you must cultivate to find true fulfilment and a sense of your own life having a core
- » The Moon—she represents your emotional needs and

tells you what you need to do in order to nurture yourself. She is essential to a feeling of being 'ok' in life.

» Saturn—this planet shows where our greatest fears lie and where we should consciously strive to achieve and overcome then. This will aid us immensely in having a strong sense of self, who is able to face the world without worry or doubt.

» The nodal axis—this is an essential pair of points in the birth chart indicating our key developmental path in life.

Now, how do we go about putting all this information together?

We might use the following template in order to come up with a True Self profile. We can then assess all the information and extract any key themes that emerge. This is essential work in preparation for meeting a soul-mate!

My approach to life is one that is (1. insert three words that represent your Ascendant sign). The issues I may have to deal with on my life's journey are (2. insert three themes that go with your Ascendant sign).

To find a core sense of identity I should cultivate qualities of (3. insert three qualities that represent your Sun-sign). I will find greatest fulfilment by exploring the arena of (4. insert a description of the house where your Sun is placed).

In order to nurture myself I should allow myself to be (5. insert three words describing your Moon-sign). On a daily basis I will feel nourished by focusing on (6. insert a description of the house your Moon is in).

My greatest fears may concern (7. insert a description of the house that Saturn is in). I may express any fears or insecurities by being (8. insert qualities that reflect your Saturn sign—this may be the more 'negative' expression of the sign or an excess of one of the 'positive' factors). Consciously working on these issues will aid me in building a stronger sense of self.

My key developmental path is connected with being (9. insert qualities of your North Node sign) and exploring them in the area of life of (10. insert North Node house). This will ultimately enable me to express my natural gifts in (11. insert qualities of South Node sign) in the sphere of (12. insert South Node house).

Once you have completed your True Self profile you can analyse it to see if any common themes occur and use it to create a plan of action for yourself.

You may be able to fill in the necessary gaps in the profile from your reading to date, and what you have already learnt about yourself and astrology. However, if that seems difficult you may like to refer to the keyword and themes glossary at the end of this chapter.

We will work through a few examples here to illustrate the process.

Suppose we have Ascendant in Cancer, Sun in Capricorn in the 7th house, Moon in Gemini in the 12th house, Saturn in Leo in the 3rd house, the North Node in Libra in the 4th house and the South Node in Aries in the 10th house.

The unique True Self profile would then look something like this:

My approach to life is one that is sensitive, emotional and imaginative. The issues I may have to deal with on my life's journey are home, family and mother.

To find a core sense of identity I should cultivate qualities of responsibility, longevity and mastery. I will find greatest fulfilment by exploring the arena of one-to-one relationships.

In order to nurture myself I should allow myself to be inquisitive, changeable and expressive. On a daily basis I will feel nourished by focusing on time alone and meditation.

My greatest fears may concern intellectual achievement or my ability to communicate. I may express any fears or insecurities by being over proud, dramatic or self-centred. Consciously working on these issues will aid me in building a stronger sense of self.

My key developmental path is connected with being diplomatic, fair and just, and exploring them in the area of life of home, family and inner experience. This will ultimately enable me to express my natural gifts in initiative, dynamism and action in the sphere of career and public status.

We see that a few themes have come from this profile. With Cancer on the Ascendant this woman will face questions about home, family and emotional experience in her life's journey. This theme is repeated by the North Node's position in the 4th house which similarly asks to look within, to concentrate on the personal sphere, rather than firstly out into the world.

Relationships are also very emphasised by the Sun's placement in the 7th house and the North Node being in Libra, again suggesting that the personal and domestic spheres of life require most focus (note that this does not mean she will not have a career—it simply means that will take care of itself if she focuses on those areas that are most important as shown by her chart).

Communication is also a theme. The Moon is in Gemini suggesting an essential emotional need to express and exchange ideas. Yet Saturn is placed in the 3rd house, which could bring fears around such matters.

A plan of action for this woman might involve taking a course on improving communication skills or an academic course that allows her to find a sense of achievement. She might also wish to consider training as a consultant or counsellor; this will fulfil her 7th house Sun, allow her to focus on the inner realm (particularly if it is counselling which deals with feelings) and also at the same time allow her to practice communication skills. She might need to ensure however that she has plenty of time alone and away from the demands of others in daily life, as the Moon's placement in the 12th house suggests this would be essential for basic nourishment.

Now we may take a second example. Suppose we have a man with Leo on the Ascendant, Sun in Sagittarius in the 5th house, Moon in Aries in the 9th house, Saturn in Aries in the 9th house, the North Node in Taurus in the 10th house and the South Node in Scorpio in the 4th house.

The unique True Self profile will then look something like this:

My approach to life is one that is confident, playful and dramatic. The issues I may have to deal with on my life's journey are being creative, and feeling special and unique.

To find a core sense of identity I should cultivate qualities of vision, faith and optimism. I will find greatest fulfilment by exploring the arena of creativity and joy in being myself.

In order to nurture myself I should allow myself to be assertive, independent and dynamic. On a daily basis I will feel nourished by focusing on religion, philosophy and wider views of life.

My greatest fears may concern religion, philosophy and wider views of life. I may express any fears or insecurities by being over energetic, self-focused or impatient. Consciously working on these issues will aid me in building a stronger sense of self.

My key developmental path is connected with being stable, peaceful and tranquil and exploring these qualities in the area of life of career and public status. This will ultimately enable me to express my natural gifts in being intense, deep and probing in the sphere of home, family and inner life.

A few themes have again immediately arisen from the analysis. We find that this man has as part of his life journey a need to be creative and feel special (as Leo is on the Ascendant). This is picked up by the Sun's placement in the 5th house which is all about fulfilment through self-expression and creativity.

Faith, religion and higher meaning is also a very important theme. The Sun is in Sagittarius and the Moon is in the 9th house, suggesting a sense of faith and view of the bigger picture brings great nurturing and fulfilment. Yet Saturn is also placed in the 9th suggesting this could be an area of fear and difficulty. Addressing his spiritual faith and wider view of the world is therefore essential for this man.

An action plan would be to start creative interests as soon as possible, whatever allows him to really express his nature. The second goal would be to consciously explore his view of God/Goddess or religion and to find some framework that nourishes him and allows him a serious yet supportive set of beliefs from which to live by.

As a third example suppose we have a woman with Ascendant in Virgo, Sun in Gemini in the 10th house, Moon in Gemini in the 10th house, Saturn in Cancer in the 11th house, the North Node in Scorpio in the 3rd house and the South Node in Taurus in the 9th house.

The unique True Self profile will then look something like this:

My approach to life is one that is diligent, organised and analytical. The issues I may have to deal with on my life's journey are service and understanding the mind-body connection.

To find a core sense of identity I should cultivate qualities of curiosity, lightness and wit. I will find greatest fulfilment by exploring the area of career, status and public life.

In order to nurture myself I should allow myself to be inquisitive, playful and sparkling. On a daily basis I will feel nourished by focusing on career, status and public life.

My greatest fears may concern community, friends or collective situations. I may express any fears or insecurities by being oversensitive, moody or emotional. Consciously working on these issues will aid me in building a stronger sense of self.

My key developmental path is connected with dealing with transformation, crisis and emotional engagement and exploring them in the area of life of learning and communication. This will ultimately enable me to express my natural gifts in being stable, practical and tranquil in the sphere of higher understanding, travel and philosophy.

There is a great deal of emphasis for this woman on the life of the mind. The Sun and Moon are both placed in Gemini, a sign which has to be inquisitive and mentally stimulated, the Ascendant is in careful and rational Virgo and the North Node asks for a transformation in learning and communication. This suggests that attending to learning, to the development of the mind, could be highly fulfilling and important. A new course of study or communication skills practice might be initial avenues to try. Career is clearly also extremely important, and it is vital this woman is able to put energy and time into her vocation and role in the world. Learning to feel more comfortable in groups could also be very beneficial and fits in with the idea of taking a course—two birds with one stone!

Your True Self profile is a summary of your major astrological placements. But it should not just remain a summary! Use it to plan some activities or new directions in your life that are really going to aid you in expressing your full nature. This will greatly enhance your chances of meeting a soul-mate who fits you as you truly are.

Key word and themes glossary

For inserts 1, 3, 5, 9, 11 you require some words describing the relevant zodiac sign. For insert 8 the words in brackets may be more appropriate. You may wish to choose from the following:

- » Aries—bravery, initiative, courage, being a pioneer, enthusiasm, energy, drive, passion (brash, hasty, selfish, aggressive)
- » Taurus—stability, peace, tranquillity, security, serenity, beauty, accumulation, practical (lazy, stuck, stubborn)
- » Gemini—inquisitiveness, curiosity, interest, sparkle, lightness, playfulness, wit (superficial, gossipy, scattered)
- » Cancer—sensitivity, imagination, attention to feeling, security, nurturing, remembering, holding (moody, over-emotional, clingy)
- » Leo—drama, faith, heart, self-expression, creativity, boldness, pride, warmth (self-centred, proud, haughty, over-dramatic)

- » Virgo—diligence, discrimination, organisation, specific skills, craft, analysis, application, intelligence (critical, fussy, nitpicking)
- » Libra—patience, diplomacy, tact, grace, style, fairness, justice, consideration, calm, arbitration, equality, balance (indecisive, lazy, vain)
- » Scorpio—intensity, transformation, depth, engagement, analysis, power, catharsis, will, probing (ruthless, vicious, paranoid)
- » Sagittarius—freedom, being a seeker, vision, energy, future-orientated, understanding, finding meaning (scattered, dogmatic, bombastic)
- » Capricorn—seriousness, mastery, discipline, integrity, ambition, longevity, tenacity, pragmatism (miserable, pessimistic, controlling)
- » Aquarius—openness, independence, logic, rationality, progressive outlook, compassion, equality, liberty (over-detached, air-headed, cold)
- » Pisces—inspiration, imagination, flow, attention to dreams, compassion, sacrifice, vision (chaotic, deceitful, evasive)

For insert 2 you will require themes relating to each zodiac sign. You may like to refer to the following ideas:

- » Aries: taking initiative, going one's own way, leaping into the unknown, becoming a warrior or adventurer
- » Taurus: building something of lasting value, collating resources, cultivating beauty, finding peace

- » Gemini: exercising the mind, duality, the dark twin, siblings, scattered energy
- » Cancer: home, mother, family, the emotions, nurturing, attending to one's moods
- » Leo: pride, developing confidence, shining as a unique individual, creativity, courage
- » Virgo: developing discrimination, understanding the mind-body connection, rational analysis, service
- » Libra: understanding justice, developing balance, creating harmony, finding style
- » Scorpio: dealing with crisis, transformation, deep emotional engagement, cutting through the surface
- » Sagittarius: exploration, finding meaning, seeking truth, embracing experience, journeying
- » Capricorn: staying the course, shouldering responsibility, cultivating reliability, climbing the mountain
- » Aquarius: embracing humanity, developing independence, becoming progressive, being over-detached
- » Pisces: flowing with life, finding inspiration, opening to other dimensions, embracing wholeness

For inserts 4, 6, 7, 10, 12 you require some words describing the relevant astrological house. You may wish to choose from the following:

- » House 1: identity, approach, physical well-being
- » House 2: resources, money, possessions, self-value
- » House 3: learning, communication, local environment, siblings

- » House 4: home, family, father, private sphere, inner life
- » House 5: creativity, recreation, joy, self-expression
- » House 6: work, service, ritual, routine, health
- » House 7: relationships, partnerships, significant others
- » House 8: shared finances, investments, intimacy, transformation, crisis
- » House 9: philosophy, religion, travel, expansion of the mind
- » House 10: career, status, public life, mother
- » House 11: community, friends, shared joy, society
- » House 12: solitude, sanctuary, spiritual connection, places on the outskirts of life

Part 3

Understanding Your Relationship Needs

Now that we have explored the central features that make up your astrological chart, and assembled your True Self profile, we will move on to the areas of the chart that specifically talk about your relationships. This will help you to understand what you really need in partnership or at least the outlines of what you are looking for. With this awareness you will be able to select a partner, or attract one to you, that best fits your own relationship requirements.

Chapter 9 will consider the Descendant, Chapter 10 Venus, Chapter 11 the 7th house and chapter 12 the Moon once again, but more from a relationship perspective. In chapter 13 we will then put together your unique Relationship Needs profile, which will combine the information you have gathered thus far in this section.

Chapter 9

Your Partnership Sign

*Y*our partnership sign is the one that is opposite your Ascendant sign. This is called the Descendant, and forms the cusp of the area of the chart that is connected with partnership. It shows the qualities that are furthest away from yourself, and therefore what you may seek in 'the other'. It may be hard to avoid seeking these qualities in a partner, although your partner certainly does not need to be the same sign as shown on your Descendant. They simply need to be able to represent in some sense the symbolic flavour of that sign.

Before each Descendant we will briefly review the Ascendant sign, so that you can see how the signs operate in pairs. Remember that the Ascendant says something about how you fundamentally are and the Descendant what you seek out in the world through those you interact with.

Ascendant in Aries, Descendant in Libra

With Aries rising, you see the world as a place of challenge, somewhere to be conquered. You approach things with a spirit of dynamism and initiative and may leap out into life, sometimes a little too hastily. With this sign on the Ascendant, you best view life as an adventure, a hero's quest. You may need to be careful of being a little too naïve sometimes but your natural courage will take you far.

In relationships you seek the balance that your go-getting nature requires. You may wish for a partner who is the epitome of harmony, balance and grace. You may see yourself as the one who chases and pursues and have very romantic ideas about wooing and charming a mate. In essence the meaning of Libra on the Descendant is for you to develop your own qualities of harmony, diplomacy and balance, for these are not ones that come most naturally.

Ascendant in Taurus, Descendant in Scorpio

Taurus on the Ascendant suggests that you see the world as a place that needs to be tackled in practical terms, brick by brick and stone by stone. You are a wonderful builder in terms of gradually increasing your sense of security in the world and your nature is basically peaceful and placid.

It is in relationships however that you may seek a deep emotional connection, as you desire to engage with another in a profound partnership that touches the depths of your soul. You may need to be careful of over-possessiveness or jealousy with this sign on the Descendant, and cultivating your own emotional depth, without a partner initially, may help you to attain equilibrium.

Ascendant in Gemini, Descendant in Sagittarius

Gemini rising gives an outlook of youth and vibrancy. You are butterfly like in your interests and have a light, inquisitive view onto the world. Intellectual and social stimulation is very important to your path through life and you benefit from new interests or courses of study.

Sagittarius on the Descendant suggests that you seek in the other someone who expands your world. Relationships that help you grow and increase your understanding of the broad principles of life are nourishing to you. Developing your own philosophy and overall system of meaning may help to take the pressure off a partner.

Ascendant in Cancer, Descendant in Capricorn

Cancer on the Ascendant suggests an approach to life that is imbued with sensitivity and imagination. It can however be somewhat timid as you cautiously approach new situations and people in a sideways manner, not wanting to be too direct. Issues of mother, home and family may be central to your life's journey.

Capricorn on the Descendant may indicate that what you seek in another is long-term security, a father or mother figure perhaps who seems to be there through thick and thin and who is able to provide a safe and practical haven away from the emotional ups and downs of your own nature. Learning to parent yourself and provide your own material security may be important in taking pressure off relationships in that sphere.

Ascendant in Leo, Descendant in Aquarius

With Leo rising, life is a stage and you were born to be at the centre of it. You have a natural love of drama and show and may approach life with generosity and faith. Being creative and self-expressive is important to your nature and 'putting yourself out there' can be important to your life's journey.

In contrast in the other you may seek someone more detached, who is open-minded and has a humanitarian streak, often thinking of the welfare of the group. You may enjoy a partner who has an intellectual or progressive streak, and who recognises the importance of freedom and breathing space in a relationship. Cultivating such qualities in yourself adds complexity to your nature.

ASCENDANT IN VIRGO, DESCENDANT IN PISCES

Virgo rising suggests a careful, analytical approach to life. You may like to take small steps forward, digesting each chunk of experience before you proceed further. This sign gives a great deal of intelligence in applied knowledge and you are able to manifest your ideas in the world. Issues of service and health may be important in your life's journey.

Pisces on the Descendant may suggest that it is in relationships where you let your barriers down. It seems that you want to merge fully with another in a sort of cosmic union. You can be very impressionable where others are concerned, perhaps wishing to save another or to somehow sacrifice yourself for the well-being of your partner. Developing your own mystical and creative side can take some pressure from your relationships.

ASCENDANT IN LIBRA, DESCENDANT IN ARIES

With Libra on the Ascendant you approach life with charm, grace and balance. You love to weigh up the pros and cons of decisions and to be seen as fair and just. Issues of justice and harmony may be central to your life's journey.

In contrast in partnerships you seek someone more dynamic and go-getting. You may like to be chased and pursued and to have a partner with much energy and fire. Becoming more dynamic and initiatory can be helpful to balance your nature even further!

Ascendant in Scorpio, Descendant in Taurus

With Scorpio rising you approach life from a suspicious viewpoint. You see the depth in everything and you are also aware instinctually of the underlying motivations of the people around you. You may be ruthless in walking your life's path but you are also highly sensitive. You engage deeply on an emotional level with the world around you and may seek crisis in which to find personal transformation and catharsis.

Taurus on the Descendant suggests you want a stable partner who can bring a sense of peace and tranquillity to your life. You need a rock to depend on, someone to act as a ballast against your crisis-prone personality. Developing steadiness and concern for the practical and material aspects of life can help to take the pressure off your partnerships.

Ascendant in Sagittarius, Descendant in Gemini

Sagittarius rising brings life as a journey to the fore. You value all your vast range of experiences along life's highway and are forever in search of meaning and the bigger picture. You are confident and have wide interests. There may be something about you that is larger than life and you need to be expanded on all levels in order to feel you are making progress through life.

Gemini on the Descendant suggests that in a partner you may seek someone who focuses your vast interests into tighter form, who is able to analyse and dissect your broad ideas. You may find yourself often with 'two' love interests or partners and cultivating your own duality and complex nature may be the key to a more settled relationship existence.

Ascendant in Capricorn, Descendant in Cancer

With Capricorn rising, life can seem a harsh and difficult place to be, a wasteland that has to be traversed. This can be a tricky sign to live rising but you make steady progress in life if you keep your self-confidence up and keep going. Eventually you are someone who can achieve great things with steady hard work.

In contrast in partnership you are much softer and long for an emotional connection where you can express a more vulnerable side to yourself. You may become attached to a partner and even dependent on them quite easily so being kinder to yourself and aware of your own vulnerability can enhance your partnerships as the pressure is then taken off a relationship.

Ascendant in Aquarius, Descendant in Leo

Aquarius rising suggests an approach to life that is detached, even scientific in a sense. You are open-minded, progressive and a natural humanitarian. You may rationalise your experience of life and awareness of the problems of humanity may be important in your life's journey.

In contrast, with Leo on the Descendant you may seek someone special who is just for you, someone who brings out your dramatic and playful side. You may lavish affection on a partner and love to show them off to others. Finding your own sense of drama and fun can be helpful on the path to integration.

Ascendant in Pisces, Descendant in Virgo

With Pisces rising, life can seem chaotic and confusing. You approach life with great intuition and compassion but may struggle with being practical or keeping your feet on the ground. A natural mystic, you may love to escape to a fantasy realm. Finding appropriate escapist outlets, such as through Art or a developed spiritual sense, is important in your life's journey.

With Virgo on the Descendant, partners who can aid you with all the practical details will be attractive. You like someone hardworking, someone with integrity and intelligence. Cultivating your own sense of being able to deal with the practical aspects of knowledge can be a positive step for you.

Now that you understand something of your partnership sign, you may like to reflect on whether past partners have offered similar qualities to the one described. To what extent were they providing this energy in your life? How could you bring those qualities more into your own way of being or into your life, so that you do not necessarily have to find them 'out there'? Some practical suggestions for finding the energy of your partnership sign for yourself are given below:

Aries as partnership sign: become more adventurous; see yourself as a hero; start something off; be sure you are voicing your own wants and needs.

Taurus as a partnership sign: cultivate stability and security in your life; be careful with your finances and start to deposit savings if you have not done so already; pay attention to your physical and material well-being, spend time in nature.

Gemini as a partnership sign: find the side of you that is sparkling, interesting and playful; treat your mind to some new ideas; take a mini-course of study or spend enough time chatting to friends and neighbours; logically analyse your beliefs.

Cancer as a partnership sign: give yourself some nurturing; create a secure and cosy home for yourself; get in touch with family and close friends; spend some time remembering positive experiences from the past; pay attention to your emotions.

Leo as a partnership sign: allow yourself to be dramatic and playful; try being the centre of attention for a while; do something creative for pure self-expression; take pride in yourself and achievements.

Virgo as a partnership sign: enjoy sorting out any messy situations in your life; weed out that which you no longer need and tidy up around you; try to be as efficient and hardworking as possible; carefully analyse your experience.

Libra as a partnership sign: try to understand other peoples' points of view; spend some time cultivating your own style or decorating your environment; feel beautiful and graceful; find your own sense of justice and balance.

Scorpio as a partnership sign: find your own intensity; let go of things and people in your life that are negative influences; psychoanalyse yourself for a week; find the depths of your emotions and desires.

Sagittarius as a partnership sign: find your own philosophy of life; travel; be open-minded; take courses in different understandings of the world; fit all your ideas into one grand scheme; get outdoors into vast open spaces.

Capricorn as a partnership sign: take control of your own finances; be your own support and rock in life; parent yourself;

find your ambitions and go after them with dedication; embrace your responsibilities.

Aquarius as a partnership sign: join a group that does something positive for society or which expresses your ideals; make time for friends; consider how you can be a better citizen; open your mind to progressive or technological advances.

Pisces as a partnership sign: spend time listening to music or another activity that takes you way from day to day reality; find inspiration; pray and meditate; be open to flowing with life.

Because your partnership sign always says something about what you find in others, the more you try and cultivate that sign in yourself, the more likely it might be that you meet a partner whilst doing so! This is because there will always be something of the partnership sign in your soul-mate. Thus, in following activities associated with that sign you have greater chance of meeting that person who will provide the best match for you at the current time.

CHAPTER 10

YOUR STYLE OF RELATIONSHIP

*V*ENUS, IDENTIFIED WITH THE GREEK goddess Aphrodite, is the planet of love and relationships. In our birth chart she says much about the style and form of relationship we may enjoy, and the kind of individual that we may be interested in attracting. Understanding our Venus is therefore an essential component of fully appreciating our relationship needs.

The philosophy of this book is that two people being fully themselves can come together in a mature, loving connection. To a degree then, it does not matter if your Venus sign is very different from that of your prospective partner. What matters rather is that the style of relationship you want can be fulfilled by the other person. This might be possible even if their Venus sign is very different, because their full nature is more complex than one planet in one sign. We will however briefly examine Venus-sign compatibility during this chapter. Being aware of your potential soul-mate's Venus sign and the style of relationship they prefer, in addition to your own preferences, may aid you in constructing a relationship that suits both of you.

First we will consider Venus through the signs and what that says about your own requirements in a relationship.

Venus in Aries

This shows that relationships for you need to be passionate, adventurous and full of initiative. It suits you to take the lead in wooing your partner and in displays of affection. Getting out and trying new things will aid your feeling of satisfaction with your partnership. This is an exciting sign for partnership and the first rush of a relationship may be the phase to which you are particularly attracted. You may therefore need to work harder on staying with a partnership once the initial excitement has worn off. Be creative in how you then spice up your romance, and take the lead in doing so. The more you can be in the driving seat in a partnership, the more you will be expressing your vital needs in this area. A fairly strong Venus sign may be required to match you, and we will discuss this further below.

Venus in Taurus

Peace, tranquillity and harmony are the name of the game here. You require stability and security in your relationships and may find a partner who somehow embodies these qualities particularly attractive. You value the tangible and the material and your relationships will benefit from fine dining, flowers and sensual accompaniments. This is a strong placement for attracting partners who have a stable, rock-like component to their nature.

It is quite unlikely that you will enjoy someone flighty or too changeable; the peacefulness in your nature would find that quite unsettling. It is also likely that you will like a partner who is settled, who understands the material world, and who has some talent in dealing with it. Perhaps your ideal partner will have their own property for example, and a healthy bank balance. This is not because you are more interested in money than love; it is simply that you love a person who has the ability to deal with the material side of life and to create a solid aura of security.

Venus in Gemini

This is quite a restless Venus. It is very important that your relationships provide intellectual stimulation and great communication. Having a partner with whom it is difficult to talk or with whom there is a lack of verbal exchange would not suit you at all. Make your relationships interesting: share ideas and books and do plenty of socialising together. Gemini is known as the sign of duality so with this sign, one may enjoy a partner with a complex character, who has two different sides to them. Venus in Gemini will also enjoy a lot of freedom in relationships, so a partner who is constantly checking up on where you are or who wants to be with you twenty-four seven is not likely to appeal. Room to breathe and enjoy reflection on the relationship will be a joy and ensures the partnership is kept alive by freshness and sparkle when you do get together.

Venus in Cancer

With Venus in Cancer you like a cosy relationship, one that makes you feel emotionally secure. You wish to be close to your partner and domestic arrangements will be important to you. Although to some extent this depends on other chart factors it is likely you will enjoy living with your partner and also be interested in constructing a family with them, even if this entails cats or dogs rather than actual children! Venus in Cancer is a placement that like Venus in Taurus will not generally be content with a flighty or too adventurous partner. Security is a major consideration, and it is important for Venus in Cancer to select a mate wisely, because they may quickly become dependent on their beloved, and find it very hard to withdraw from their own emotional involvement.

Venus in Leo

Here you love to lavish affection on your beloved and may become very focused on one person. You must feel proud of your partner and you enjoy a relationship with plenty of glamour and show. Your relationships may suffer if there is too much everyday pressure on them, for example with house chores. Instead ensure there are plenty of nights out and weekends away in (ideally) expensive hotels. For Venus in Leo romance is a grand affair; this is the placement of a great lover, one who really enjoys the feeling of being in love with one special person. The relationships of a Venus in Leo person must honour the regal quality and style of the individual; some luxury in love is required.

Venus in Virgo

With this placement you may have very exacting standards for your relationship. You enjoy a partnership that has a quiet, modest feel but which is full of integrity and which respects each of your working commitments. Routines and rituals may be important in your partnerships and a partner who respects this is essential. This is a Venus who may be quite particular about her relationships, and who may specify just what they should be like. Criticising one's partner or being over-fussy could be an issue, as could an overly moralistic point of view. Yet you are likely to be considerate and kind for the majority of the time, and see an element of service at work in your connection with the other person.

Venus in Libra

Venus in Libra suggests you like your relationships to be full of courtly style and grace. You are likely to enjoy wining and dining and appreciate flowers and perfume; basically, all the trappings of romance. For you the other is very important and you will be quite idealistic about your partner and insist on them being well presented. Your relationships benefit from harmony and equality in all matters. This is a very stylish Venus, and one that may easily attract potential suitors. Making decisions about love could be a more difficult task for you, as you do enjoy reflecting on both ends of a dilemma, and weighing them up carefully. A relationship with too much mundane reality or which leaves no room for hearts and flowers may be rather draining for you. Beauty is important to you, and your relationships will benefit from any small touches of style you are able to include in your day to day routine. It may also be very important to have a relationship of equality, where both partners are seen as equals. Even though you are usually romantic, the old stereotyped roles of male and female are unlikely to appeal; total balance in your connection will be sought.

Venus in Scorpio

With Venus in Scorpio you enjoy intense connections with other people that are quite sexual and emotionally engaging. Jealousy and possessiveness can be a problem with this placement although on the positive side you can be extremely loyal and are capable of relationships which can undergo some very testing periods. In fact now and again you may enjoy a crisis! Ensure you connect with someone who is sufficiently engaging on an emotional level for your taste. Relationships are a serious business for you and you will want a partner who is able to give a lot to you, especially by way of trust and commitment in emotional issues. You may be prone to analysing your partnership a little too intensely so withdrawing occasionally can be quite helpful, as could allowing them some breathing space. Because you are innately suspicious when it comes to your lover, it is important to choose someone who will not exacerbate this tendency in any way, for example by flirting with others, even if they meant nothing beyond a surface connection.

Venus in Sagittarius

With this placement you enjoy relationships that have a quality of freedom about them and which promote growth and new horizons. This can sometimes be problematic for conventional domestic set-ups but all you need to do is ensure you select a partner who has sufficiently broad interests, and is prepared to give you the freedom you need. Relationships with partners from different cultures may be attractive, as would travel abroad together. Venus in Sagittarius is a lively, fun placement for Venus, easily bored and restless. It could be difficult for you to be with someone who enjoys a more conventional or secure set-up in a relationship, as for you part of love's attraction is in its future possibilities. This suggests that formal commitment might be tricky, unless there are a lot of counter indications in your birth chart, as the narrowing of future options is not something that is likely to make your heart sing! The key here perhaps is to ensure sufficient adventure and growth potential within any partnership you enter.

Venus in Capricorn

Venus in Capricorn enjoys relationships that are serious, mature and last for a long time. You will like a partner who has a realistic understanding of the world and is able to achieve things in a material sense. Ambitious or successful partners are also attractive. Sometimes an older partner can be suitable for you as you are often able to relate to those with greater experience and maturity than that of your own age group. With Venus in Capricorn you will like a partner who is dignified and well-organised, someone who turns up when they say they will, and who does what they say they will do. This is probably the strongest Venus sign for formal commitments, such as marriage or other relationship contracts, as there is something about you that enjoys the social structure surrounding a relationship. Once you know you are in it for the long-term you can relax some of the natural control of your nature, and express the strong affections lying within.

Venus in Aquarius

This Venus requires relationships that are egalitarian and progressive. Any relationship you have must accord with your wider principles and be very democratic. An old-fashioned wife/husband relationship where the wife does all the domestic chores for example is unlikely to appeal. It is very important to you that your relationships contain sufficient intellectual stimulation and allow both of you to pursue your own interests. Joining a group or society together may also appeal as your relationships often have a wider focus than the purely personal. With Venus in Aquarius independence is important to you, and you must have room to breathe and be your own person. Taking time away from your partner will often be a welcome space in which you can pursue your own lofty ideals. Friendship is often a very important aspect of relationship with this placement, and beginning relationships as friends is often the way partnerships start for you.

Venus in Pisces

With Venus in Pisces you may sometimes be overwhelmed by a general love of humanity. You are very fluid in your relationships and may sometimes struggle to maintain a boundary between you and the other person. Relationships which inspire you and which allow you to escape from everyday matters may appeal greatly. You may also sometimes be attracted to those who need saving in some way, and this is a tendency to be wary of, just in case your kind nature is sometimes taken advantage of. Ensure your relationships are full of romance and mysticism (whatever that may mean to you and even if you are not 'religious' or 'spiritual'). With Venus in Pisces relationships may sometimes also be an area of confusion for you, or you can be so focused on your own dreams of romance that you manage to miss the real person in front of you. Although you are emotional and sensitive in love, you also have a strong need for flexibility, so a relationship that is too tightly constructed may have you slipping out of the back door when nobody is looking.

Before we look at the house placement of Venus we are going to consider the issue of Venus-sign compatibility. This can be important for relationships as if two people fundamentally disagree on the style of a relationship, how it is going to operate, then it is unlikely that the relationship will be able to last beyond the initial attraction period. Whilst it is never the case that you cannot be with someone with a very different Venus sign, it is worth understanding where they are coming from so that you can ensure both sets of needs are met in the partnership.

If you have the same Venus sign as your prospective partner then you will immediately have similar views on how to conduct the relationship. We will not therefore consider Venus in Aries with Venus in Aries or Venus in Leo with Venus in Leo, for example.

Venus in Aries, Venus in Taurus

With this pair Venus in Aries will like initiative, action and adventure in the relationship whilst Venus in Taurus will be more focused on security and stability. To make it work, both may have to compromise and neither is very good at this! This could be a tricky one to manage, with creative solutions required.

Venus in Aries, Venus in Gemini

Here we have two Venus signs who enjoy a stimulating relationship. Both are prepared to entertain an adventurous streak in the connection, and even if Venus in Gemini won't actually take the action, it is prepared to talk about it! There could be good compatibility here.

Venus in Aries, Venus in Cancer

This could be a tricky combination, as Venus in Aries will love independence just as much as Venus in Cancer loves dependence! Unless one is prepared to play the initiator and adventurer whilst the other stays home in the safety of the shared nest, there could be some difficult negotiations as regards shared activities.

Venus in Aries, Venus in Leo

These two fiery signs should understand each other well. Both like a relationship with a bit of energy, zest and enthusiasm and neither will be afraid of showing the world that's the way it is.

Venus in Aries, Venus in Virgo

These two have very different conceptions of a relationship. Venus in Aries focuses on passion and adventure whilst Venus in Virgo on the details and practical aspects. This is not a natural match, and could take some work to sort out.

Venus in Aries, Venus in Libra

These two are opposites and with Venus in Aries exuberantly charging ahead in partnership, Venus in Libra could be left wondering what on earth is going on, as it tries to weigh up the best option. Venus in Aries may be too thoughtless and headstrong in partnership for Venus in Libra to handle, and just not as refined as Venus in Libra would like.

Venus in Aries, Venus in Scorpio

This could be an interesting match. Both these signs are ruled by Mars, and there is a spirit of the warrior about both. This could be a passionate, tempestuous couple, with Venus in Scorpio demanding Venus in Aries' attention. Fireworks could fly, but it could be interesting!

Venus in Aries, Venus in Sagittarius

Two fire signs again, so there is innate understanding as to the basic energy of a relationship. Venus in Sagittarius could be quite restless for Venus in Aries' taste but both understand the need for vision and creativity in forging a successful partnership.

Venus in Aries, Venus in Capricorn

Both these signs share a love of ambition and drive, and they may understand each other in terms of wanting a partnership that allows these things to flourish. Venus in Aries may become bored however by Venus in Capricorn's liking for duty and commitment, unless it can see these things as adventures in themselves.

Venus in Aries, Venus in Aquarius

This could be a good match. Both love independence and freedom within partnership which might suggest they spend more time apart than together! But when they do return to each other they are likely to bring originality and spark.

Venus in Aries, Venus in Pisces

This is an unusual match but one that could work. Venus in Aries will love doing its own thing in relationship but Venus in Pisces also loves to slip away now and then, to escape into its own world. Venus in Aries is likely to be active whilst Venus in Pisces may be more passive in the connection. Values are unlikely to match but there is some scope here for understanding.

Venus in Taurus, Venus in Gemini

These two may get along to a degree although Venus in Taurus will enjoy a relationship that has stable and clear rules and practices, whereas Venus in Gemini will enjoy something more spontaneous, even light, which does not get too heavy or bogged down in material matters.

Venus in Taurus, Venus in Cancer

These two will understand each other well. Both value security and the domestic environment in their partnerships, and Venus in Taurus could be a welcome fortress for the emotional Venus in Cancer.

Venus in Taurus, Venus in Leo

These two both understand the need for a strong, firm relationship, and could both be quite committed, having good staying power. Both may be stubborn so that could be an issue, but generally this could be a good pairing, with the quieter Venus in Taurus enjoying the louder and more showy Venus in Leo. Both have a liking for material comfort, which is also an added bonus.

Venus in Taurus, Venus in Virgo

These two will understand each other in terms of both being pragmatic and understanding the practical dimensions of a relationship. Yet Venus in Taurus will value comfort and security whereas Venus in Virgo may be more concerned with efficiency and a relationship that conforms to specific standards. The hardworking values of Venus in Virgo may be a little much for more relaxed Venus in Taurus, who enjoys more time to indulge in sensual pleasures.

Venus in Taurus, Venus in Libra

These two Venus-ruled signs will both understand a need for beauty and harmony in a relationship. They may both enjoy a comfortable, aesthetic environment, which allows them to indulge in sensuous pleasure and artistic concerns. This is a good pairing, with two considerate and charming partners.

Venus in Taurus, Venus in Scorpio

These two are opposite in the zodiac, but have much in common. Both will enjoy a stable connection that allows strong focus on the relationship and both will have strong physical/sexual needs, although Venus in Taurus may be more sensual and Venus in Scorpio more overtly sexual. This is a strong pairing however, a case of 'opposites attract'.

Venus in Taurus, Venus in Sagittarius

These two are not a natural pairing. Venus in Sagittarius loves freedom and a relationship that expands and grows whereas Venus in Taurus will be much more content with preserving a good quality connection already in existence. Some work will need to be done to construct a good relationship from both perspectives.

Venus in Taurus, Venus in Capricorn

This is a good match. Each understands the values of the other and each is particularly fond of material and physical comfort and pleasure.

Venus in Taurus, Venus in Aquarius

There are differences here. Both enjoy a stable relationship however; although Venus in Aquarius is very concerned with the principles of its governance whereas Venus in Taurus is more focused on the practical side. The intellectual values of Venus in Aquarius may be unfathomable for Venus in Taurus; and both may be stubborn! Thus compromise could be tricky.

Venus in Taurus, Venus in Pisces

There could be some compatibility here. Both are quiet and peaceful Venus placements. Venus in Pisces however requires something inspirational or mystical about its partnerships, whereas Venus in Taurus is more content with down to earth pleasures. A love of art could unite these two, perhaps.

Venus in Gemini, Venus in Cancer

One of these can be flighty, and has a love of intelligence and a smart, street-wise relationship (Venus in Gemini). The other is much more content with homely pleasures, enjoying the security of a strong emotional bond. If Venus in Cancer can leave Venus in Gemini to breathe now and again there might be a connection, although it's not the easiest.

Venus in Gemini, Venus in Leo

These two Venus signs are playful and affectionate. Whilst Venus in Gemini may need more space than Venus in Leo, the two may get along fairly well, enjoying each others' lively and stimulating company.

Venus in Gemini, Venus in Virgo

Both these Venus signs value thinking and the life of the mind. This could create a good partnership, where intelligent activities form part of its functioning. Venus in Virgo may sometimes be a little exacting for Venus in Gemini, but they are both flexible and may accommodate each other.

Venus in Gemini, Venus in Libra

These two are a good pairing. Both will think carefully about their relationship, and enjoy finding balance with the other.

Venus in Gemini, Venus in Scorpio

There may be a clash of values here. The freedom and breathing space needed by Venus in Gemini in a partnership may be almost offensive to Venus in Scorpio who likes to connect very intensely. If communication channels remain open, these two might make it, but it will take some effort.

Venus in Gemini, Venus in Sagittarius

This is a happy match. Both enjoy ideas and lots of conversation! They both also understand that freedom is important within a partnership and are likely to give each other plenty of space and breathing room.

Venus in Gemini, Venus in Capricorn

These two may not understand each other well. Venus in Gemini will take a lighter, less formal approach to relationships whilst Venus in Capricorn will like a serious connection that has clearly defined rules and a structure within which to operate.

Venus in Gemini, Venus in Aquarius

Another happy pairing. These two airy Venus' will enjoy a relationship based on ideas and principles, containing plenty of social stimulation and outings.

Venus in Gemini, Venus in Pisces

This is an odd pairing. These two could miss each other quite easily. Venus in Gemini likes to engage in witty conversation with its partner and Venus in Pisces might be too lost in the ether to respond. Whilst Venus in Gemini flutters off like a butterfly in one direction, Venus in Pisces may be floating down the river in the other!

Venus in Cancer, Venus in Leo

These too emotional creatures may get along quite well. If Venus in Leo adores Venus in Cancer then Venus in Cancer will quickly fall into her hero or heroine's arms. Each will have the strong, secure relationship it likes.

Venus in Cancer, Venus in Virgo

This quiet pair may understand each other well. Both may be prone to criticising the other, which may need to be watched, but both will understand the importance of care and consideration in a partnership.

Venus in Cancer, Venus in Libra

This could be a reasonable pairing. Both will like a partnership that has an element of formality, a sense of stability and safety. Venus in Libra may be more concerned with equality and will need more room to breathe but could appreciate the soft Venus in Cancer nature.

Venus in Cancer, Venus in Scorpio

These two may get along well. Both like an emotional relationship, which honours the feelings. Both may be equally possessive of the other, and together they may create a powerful bond.

Venus in Cancer, Venus in Sagittarius

This is a most unlikely pairing. The love of freedom and prioritising of friendship that Venus in Sagittarius is famed for may be quite offensive to Venus in Cancer, who loves closeness and a sense of being able to depend totally on the other.

Venus in Cancer, Venus in Capricorn

This could be a good match. Both like a conventional relationship in terms of a committed structure, and both are concerned with the importance of the home and family. These are opposites but they understand each other.

Venus in Cancer, Venus in Aquarius

Here we have a challenging pairing. The detachment of Venus in

Aquarius and its liking for a modern, progressive relationship may be wholly unfathomable to home-loving and more conventional Venus in Cancer.

Venus in Cancer, Venus in Pisces

This watery pair will understand each other on one level and both enjoy a relationship that brings out oceans of feeling. Yet Venus in Cancer's concerns are very much based around the home and security whereas Venus in Pisces loves to soar into the realm of the spirit. There may be a connection, but it is by no means certain.

Venus in Leo, Venus in Virgo

These two Venus signs will prefer very different styles of relating. Whilst Venus in Leo likes grand displays, luxurious romantic dates, and likes to splash out on the trappings of love, Venus in Virgo prefers a more modest affair, focusing on the demands of everyday life and the specifics of the connection.

Venus in Leo, Venus in Libra

These two make a fine match, with both enjoying a relationship of good style and taste. Both also enjoy displays of romance, such as flowers and fine dining, and this could be a happy connection.

Venus in Leo, Venus in Scorpio

Together, with these two, we have a dramatic pairing, but this could be a reasonable match in terms of what each wants from a relationship. Both enjoy a stable connection, and both enjoy being devoted to one another.

Venus in Leo, Venus in Sagittarius

These two understand each other's liking for a warm, energetic partnership but may not be so compatible when it comes to the issue of being focused on that one special person. Whilst for Venus in Leo this is a given, Venus in Sagittarius is rather more prone to having its options open.

Venus in Leo, Venus in Capricorn

These two both value status and ambition and could have a successful partnership, each understanding themselves as stronger in the world as a partnership than as two separate individuals. Venus in Leo will love grand gestures, and Venus in Capricorn will appreciate the style and luxury Venus in Leo brings to a relationship.

Venus in Leo, Venus in Aquarius

It is sometimes said that opposites attract, but not in this case. The warm, one special person focus of Venus in Leo is unlikely to match Venus in Aquarius' liking for a thinking partnership with many friendships and ideals about the human family as a whole.

Venus in Leo, Venus in Pisces

These two may both enjoy a partnership of glamour and romance and hence have similar likings in a relationship. Venus in Leo will however be much more straightforward, honest and open about what it wants in a relationship whereas Venus in Pisces could be maddeningly unclear.

Venus in Virgo, Venus in Libra

These two Venus signs may enjoy a similar style of partnership. Both will be considerate and quiet in their relationship demands, and enjoy perfecting the union that has arisen.

Venus in Virgo, Venus in Scorpio

These two quiet signs could get along well in partnership. Each is highly analytical and together they might have to be careful not to analyse their relationship to death!

Venus in Virgo, Venus in Sagittarius

There is something flexible about Venus in Virgo, yet it is hardly the wide-ranging flexibility of Venus in Sagittarius. These two will prefer quite different styles of relationship, although they have in common a liking for knowledge and intellectual exchange.

Venus in Virgo, Venus in Capricorn

These two understand each other well but together they may have to be careful not to let their love drown in a wellspring of efficiency and material concern. The hard-working values of each of these placements could mean romance and love get pushed to one side. Both will value honesty and integrity in a partnership, and they may be great working partners in addition to lovers.

Venus in Virgo, Venus in Aquarius

These two placements could get along well. Each would be happy in a relationship that honours the intellectual side of life and gives each room to think and pursue their own interests. Venus in Virgo will however be more inclined to put its knowledge to use, and perhaps work harder to make the relationship work. If idealistic Aquarius can make the leap to getting theory into practice, both could benefit.

Venus in Virgo, Venus in Pisces

These two may attract as opposites, but Venus in Virgo, with its liking for clear rules and routines in a partnership, may become easily frustrated by the fluidity and perhaps the unreliability of Venus in Pisces.

Venus in Libra, Venus in Scorpio

There is potential here although Venus in Libra, with its love of balance, could become frustrated by the intensity of Venus in Scorpio in relationship, and perhaps their inability to detach from the feeling side of the partnership in order to reflect.

Venus in Libra, Venus in Sagittarius

These two make a light, sociable pair, with easy-going Venus in Libra making fast friends with outgoing Venus in Sagittarius. Venus in Libra may have more conventional notions about the relationship when it comes to commitment however, and may find Venus in Sagittarius has escaped before one has even said the word 'relationship.'

Venus in Libra, Venus in Capricorn

These two may make a good match. Both like a serious relationship, and are keen on formal contracts and commitment. Both also like dignified partnerships that show good taste and style.

Venus in Libra, Venus in Aquarius

Venus in Aquarius will share Venus in Libra's love of rationally appraising any relationship they are in. They both enjoy relationships that have an aesthetic, beautiful quality. Venus in Aquarius may have more progressive ideas on the structure of the relationship but both have a strong sense of equality.

Venus in Libra, Venus in Pisces

These two both enjoy a relationship with lots of romance, although Venus in Libra's concern for perfect balance in the partnership may be undermined by slippery Venus in Pisces. For Venus in Pisces, love and adoration may involve almost a sacrifice of self, and that may upset the ideals of Venus in Libra.

Venus in Scorpio, Venus in Sagittarius

These two may have very different ideas about relationships. Venus in Scorpio demands absolute attention and engagement whilst Venus in Sagittarius must keep some element of freedom and growth to a partnership.

Venus in Scorpio, Venus in Capricorn

This could be a good match. Both understand a relationship that can withstand tough challenges, and both will stick in there through good and bad. Neither is adverse to a little difficulty in partnership if it contributes to a happy ending.

Venus in Scorpio, Venus in Aquarius

Values could clash here, with Venus in Scorpio honing in on intimate exchange with another whilst Venus in Aquarius is busy extending its circle of friends; the partner may be seen as one of these friends, which could be maddening for Venus in Scorpio.

Venus in Scorpio, Venus in Pisces

These two understand each other's need for emotional involvement although Venus in Scorpio may sometimes get too intense for Venus in Pisces, who enjoys an escape into its own fantasy world every now and then.

Venus in Sagittarius, Venus in Capricorn

These two are very different in terms of the type of relationship they will enjoy. Venus in Capricorn likes to know exactly where it stands, what the rules and form is of the partnership. Venus in Sagittarius on the other hand will not enjoy being pinned down and likes some flexibility and openness to its connection. Whilst Venus in Sagittarius may prioritise friendship, Venus in Capricorn may focus on commitment.

Venus in Sagittarius, Venus in Aquarius

These two could share many a happy date! Each has similar values of freedom and independence, and each loves a good discussion about wide-ranging concepts. Venus in Aquarius is a more stable influence in a relationship, but together in a partnership with plenty of space, these two could be very happy.

Venus in Sagittarius, Venus in Pisces

This could be an interesting partnership. Both share a love of inspiration and vision and have a periodic need to escape into their own dreams. Each may value a relationship that takes them beyond everyday concerns and together we could have a partnership of inspiration and dreams.

Venus in Capricorn, Venus in Aquarius

These two may get along surprisingly well. Each is fairly detached in its assessment of a relationship and both can be in it for the long-haul. Venus in Aquarius may be more independent and freedom-conscious than Venus in Capricorn, but they may get along well enough, if each can respect the other's position.

Venus in Capricorn, Venus in Pisces

The vagueness and unreliability of Venus in Pisces could be frustrating for Venus in Capricorn, who likes a partner who firmly understands the rules of the relationship. The idealism of Venus in Pisces may also grate, as Venus in Capricorn knows that relationships have their practical element too.

Venus in Aquarius, Venus in Pisces

These two may understand each other fairly well, with Venus in Aquarius being tolerant enough to allow Venus in Pisces to be the dreamer and romantic he or she is.

The house placement of Venus is also very important and may help you understand in which areas of life you are most concerned with relationships and even sometimes where you may meet a partner. Find the house of your Venus from your birth chart and look up its placement below.

Venus in the 1st House

With this placement relationships are a very important facet of your personality. As a naturally charming individual you may easily attract prospective partners to you. Focusing on your own style and wants in a relationship is likely to be of importance. It may also be that you value a partner who is good at initiating and who has a fairly forceful personality.

Venus in the 2nd House

With this placement your relationships play a very important part in your self-esteem. It is therefore important to choose partners who make you feel good and boost your confidence. It seems that for you relationships are also connected with your income or finances and you may well work with your partner or find that she or he has a positive impact on your financial situation.

Venus in the 3rd House

Here, relationships play a central role in your learning and communication. Taking courses or further study may be a particularly fruitful area for meeting potential partners and you value shared learning and conversations. You may also find a love match within your local environment, for example, at the local shops or park!

Venus in the 4th House

With Venus in the 4th house you love the privacy and domesticity that can be a part of some relationships. Ensuring your love can flourish in comfortable surroundings may be important to your relationship as can spending time at home together. The sharing of the inner world and family issues may also be key components of your partnerships. You may meet someone through family connections or events.

Venus in the 5th House

Here, Venus loves the joy of relating and creativity. Sharing your unique form of creativity with your partner might be high on your list of things to do in couple time. It is essential that with your partner you spend much time just enjoying each others' company, going out, and indulging in lots of 'playtime' and romantic dates. Holidays, fun and sheer enjoyment are the order of the day. Pursuing your hobbies may be how you meet your partner.

Venus in the 6th House

With Venus in the 6th house your relationships are a very important part of your daily routine. This may mean living with a partner or developing a particular timetable with your loved one that suits you both. Sharing work interests together might be important here, and ensuring you take the time each day to remind each other how much you care could be important. You may meet your partner at work or at a place that forms part of your regular routine, such as the gym.

Venus in the 7th House

Here, partnership takes on an even greater role than it usually does. You easily attract partners and have the need for creating equal and beautiful relationships. You may be particularly concerned that your relationship has the correct form, for example conforming to social norms.

Venus in the 8th House

Here your relationship needs to take you to the deeper dimensions of life. Perhaps you explore psychology together, or the occult. Your relationship needs to engage you and bring intensity to your life. Therefore you will need a serious partner who can give you the level of attention you require.

Venus in the 9th House

With Venus in the 9th house your relationship needs to take you beyond known boundaries. Exploring different philosophies or travelling abroad with your partner will be excellent ways to cultivate a relationship that satisfies your need for continual growth and expansion. Do not let your relationship become confined to a small space; allow it to be a vehicle through which you and your partner continue to develop and expand your horizons. You may meet someone far from home, for example on travels abroad or whilst you are exploring religious or philosophical views.

Venus in the 10th House

Here your relationship is closely related to your career and status in life. Your relationship must make you feel proud and that you are happy for it to be known about. You may work with your partner and forming some business together might be an excellent outlet for this placement. You may meet someone through your career.

Venus in the 11th House

With Venus in the 11th house it is essential you and your partner are good friends and that you actively involve yourselves in the community around you. Joining a group together that you are both interested in will help your relationship to flourish. Friends may be instrumental in helping you meet a partner and you may also meet someone through joining a group or collective activity.

Venus in the 12th House

Here there may be something secretive or particularly spiritual about your relationships. Taking time to meditate together or explore the deeper patterns underlying your connection will be highly beneficial. In addition, making sure you each have time alone, with sufficient space to be as you need to, could be important. You may meet someone whilst engaged in charitable activities, or in an unusual setting such as a hospital or even prison!

Having now learned about our Venus by sign and house, we can now construct a combined interpretation to gain a richer understanding of how she is functioning in our life. The examples below will aid you in making your own interpretation.

Venus in Aquarius in the 10th House

Here we enjoy relating to many friends and groups, and in a personal relationship we maintain an air of detachment and ability for rational appraisal. Independence within partnership will be important to us. We place high value on our career and it is highly likely that love will be linked with our public status. We should therefore be particularly mindful of meeting people through our work and career and look out for those whose principles accord with our own.

Venus in Pisces in the 2ⁿᵈ House

With Venus in Pisces we enjoy a relationship that allows us to encounter the divine, that provides inspiration and a means for us to express our flowing, emotional nature. We will want room to sometimes slip away in our partnership, to soar up into our own dreams and fantasies. Relationships are strongly related to our own sense of self-value and our finances. Perhaps a partner inspires us to make money for ourselves, or to improve our resources. We may meet someone whilst we are trying to improve our own financial situation.

Venus in Capricorn in the 4ᵗʰ House

Here we value a serious and committed partnership, which stands the test of time and allows us to focus on worldly ambitions and achievements. We also enjoy and value our home, property in general and our inner life. Starting a property business with a partner might be a lovely expression of this placement as could living together in a long-term union that involves plenty of introspection whilst also being focused on the demands of the material world.

We have now completed our analysis of Venus, goddess of love. An understanding of her placement in your chart is very valuable, for you now understand the style and form of relationship that will be most suitable for you. You will also be mindful of the Venus sign of any prospective soul-mates.

Chapter 11

The Place of the Other

As we have mentioned in previous chapters, there is one house in the horoscope, or one area of the chart, that is particularly connected with relationships. This is the 7th house, the place of the 'other'. The Descendant sign will always be the start of the 7th house, but matters become more complicated when you have planets in the 7th house.

Any planets placed in this area of the chart will express their energy in your partnerships. The people you meet may live out the themes they represent for example, or issues that they symbolise will be strong elements in your relationship.

It is therefore essential to consider any such planets, and integrate them into your relationship needs profile. Look at your chart and discover which, if any, planets are placed in the 7th house. Then read the interpretation below.

Sun in the 7th House

In this case your entire life purpose is bound up with relationships. It is therefore crucial to your fulfilment that you are prepared to engage with others on a one-to-one level, for only then will you truly be able to find yourself. There are some things to be careful of however. The astrological Sun is a key signifier of your identity. Thus, with this placement, there can be a tendency to give your identity away to another person. For example, if you attract a strong partner into your life, you might start to believe that they are the centre of your world and that your role in life is connected only to your relationship to them. In one sense it is absolutely true that relationships provide you with meaning and fulfilment. Yet this is a different thing to living through someone else. Therefore choose your partners with great care, and check in with yourself regularly to ensure you have not given yourself away to your partner, in the sense that you are now living through them rather than being an independent person in your own right. You should also be aware that the Sun in the 7th house may sometimes indicate that you are searching for a father figure in your partnerships; as long as you are aware of any tendencies in this direction you should be able to navigate them without too much difficulty.

Moon in the 7th House

In some ways the Moon in the 7th house is even trickier than the Sun in the 7th house. This is because your essential emotional needs are bound up with relationships; you need to be in a partnership to feel secure and right with yourself on a fundamental level. Clearly this can lead to some difficulties as regards to becoming dependent on a partner very quickly and thus suffering greatly if a relationship then comes to an end. With this placement you may also be seeking a certain amount of mothering through a relationship and again awareness of this is the key to not letting it take over a union of two independent individuals. A good strategy for dealing with the Moon in the 7th house is to cultivate close friendships that are emotionally nurturing. Relationships with women will be particularly beneficial, regardless of whether you are male or female. What you need from such friendships is ongoing emotional support. Even soul-mates may come and go in our lives, so with the Moon here, you should create a life for yourself that ensures sufficient long-term emotional support of a day-to-day variety that is unlikely to be removed from you. Family relationships with female members may also be particularly important.

Mercury in the 7th House

With Mercury in the 7th house, communication and learning through partnership becomes all important. Firstly, a partner who stimulates you on an intellectual level is essential, someone interesting, witty and youthful in spirit. Secondly however you may have a tendency to see your partner as the clever, versatile one as opposed to yourself. Planets in the 7th are very prone to projection, meaning we see in the other something that is really our own. When we give our own energies away, projecting them onto others, eventually we begin to feel a piece of our soul is missing. In this case therefore, you may wish to be extra vigilant to cultivate your own intellect and communication skills, because ultimately you have a talent for reaching other people through these means, even if that does not seem immediately obvious!

Venus in the 7th House

The benefit of Venus in the 7th house is that relationships are likely to come to you quite easily. This is the goddess of attraction in the house of the partner. You may therefore find it easy to attract potential mates and offers of partnership or even marriage. Others may see you as attractive and friendly and this exacerbates your natural charms. The difficulty here is that attracting many potential partners does not necessarily mean they are all of the highest quality! Discrimination is therefore an important lesson with this 'lucky' placement. By no means are all who come into your sphere going to be suitable or real soul-mates. So revel in your attractive qualities but cultivate awareness that some partnerships will be more suitable than others. You may also be prone to picking up the values of your partner and living them as if they were your own; again, a tendency to be aware of.

Mars in the 7th House

With the God of War in the house of partnership, some careful handling may be required. On the positive side you have a wonderful capacity for dynamic, exciting relationships that contain adventure, drive and passion. You are also much energised through your partnerships and may do particularly well in associations that have a working element. The more negative side may be that you see your partner as the one who is assertive and in the driving seat rather than yourself. This is a case of a Mars that has been given away! Here therefore being aware of any tendency to see action and dynamism in others but not yourself can be important in reconnecting with your own potency and ability to act. Taking the initiative in relationships would actually suit you very well, so make them exciting, dynamic and full of energy!

Jupiter in the 7th House

With Jupiter here your relationships have to contain an element of freedom and growth. You will enjoy partnerships that bring an expansion of your world. Travelling or exploring religion and philosophy with your partners would be an ideal outlet for this energy. If you have a routine partnership you are likely to become bored and restless and may look further afield for new avenues and adventures. It is therefore essential that you build into your relationship a sense of being able to grow together and explore the world as a team.

Saturn in the 7th House

In the house of partnership Saturn may enjoy a very serious, long-term connection with a mature partner. There could be some innate fears around relationships, perhaps feelings of insecurity or not being worthy enough to be loved by someone else. But if you can take things step by step and appreciate that you are someone who simply takes these matters more seriously than most people, you can build a lasting and satisfying relationship that has excellent structure and boundaries.

Chiron in the 7th House

Here, themes of wounding and healing come into your one to one relationships. You may attract a partner who is wise, on some level a healer, and who helps you to come to terms with difficult issues in your past. On another level you may open up your own wounds and pain through one to one relating and this can be difficult as you are forced into a deep confrontation with your own pain. Ultimately your relationships have the capacity to be areas of learning and wisdom, where you both find healing through the experience of being together.

URANUS IN THE 7TH HOUSE

With Uranus here, relationships can be surprising, excitable and full of changes. You may be awakened through partnership or have sudden experiences connected with them that take you to a whole new level of consciousness. Freedom is exceptionally important in your partnerships and you would do well to create a relationship that contains plenty of space for each of you to inhabit. Surprising your partner would also fit well with this placement. You are very unique and original in your approach to partnership and if you recognise this you can create an exciting, energised connection.

NEPTUNE IN THE 7TH HOUSE

With Neptune in the 7th house partnership can be an area of mystery! There is something intangible and alluring about your relationships. You may have a very spiritual connection, or one that is shrouded in a romantic mist, so that you feel you and your partner are destined to be together forever. Being over-idealistic or romantic may be a problem with his placement, but the positive side is that you have the capacity to create a relationship that is very strong on the spiritual level, and which enables you to truly merge as one unit.

PLUTO IN THE 7TH HOUSE

Here, Pluto will bring its penchant for crisis, destruction and regeneration into the sphere of relationships. This is likely to mean you will have intense, deep connections with others that are psychologically transformative and which penetrate the very depths of your soul. You may also be prone to engaging with others for certain powerful periods before that relationship breaks down and you emerge a new person. Once you have undergone any necessary purging in this area you will be able to create a relationship of incredible depth and emotional intensity.

Working with our 7th house planets is extremely important. We are almost bound to meet them in some form or other in our relationships and therefore being aware of their existence and possible impact in our partnerships is essential self-knowledge. The more we can live the planet in question ourselves, the less we will need to find them in another, and the more authentic our relationships will be. Some ideas for living your 7th house planets are given below:

- » Sun in the 7th house—be vigilant about your identity; shine as yourself and not through others
- » Moon in the 7th house—take back your feelings and needs; honour and nurture your emotions
- » Mercury in the 7th house—take time to consider your own opinions and to clearly communicate them to others; be careful not to be too influenced by the opinions of others
- » Venus in the 7th house—find your own beauty, style and taste; concentrate on the relationship you have with yourself
- » Mars in the 7th house—contact your own aggression and

anger; be sure to assert yourself so you do not experience anger from others

» Jupiter in the 7th house—find your own beliefs and faith in life; work out how you can expand your life without the assistance of someone else

» Chiron in the 7th house—identify any wound you feel and take steps to heal yourself and understand any learning from this process; realise that the pain you see in others may be a mirror of your own

» Saturn in the 7th house—consciously take back responsibilities and duties that belong to you, but do not take on burdens of other people that are not truly yours

» Uranus in the 7th house—find your own eccentric, genius-side; embrace your quirkiness and uniqueness

» Neptune in the 7th house—seek inspiration in your life; immerse yourself in music or poetry; find your own muse rather than seeing it in those around you

» Pluto in the 7th house—find your own power and intensity; take back your ability to transform your life from the inside-out

Now we have worked with our 7th house planets we will return to the question of the Moon, so important to our relationship life.

Chapter 12

Return to the Moon

You will recall that in chapter 5 we discussed your astrological Moon, relating it to your core needs as an individual; what you need to do each day in order to nurture and nourish yourself. In this chapter we will be returning to the idea of the Moon but focusing on what she might mean for relationships.

The Moon is extremely important in relationships, as she represents our feelings and emotional needs. We must therefore ensure she is honoured in our partnerships, as otherwise we are unlikely to be happy. In this chapter we will therefore take a further brief look at the Moon in each sign and house, with specific focus on how her needs can be met in a relationship. We will then try to synthesise some sign and house combinations.

Moon in Aries

With this Moon-sign you need independence and to focus on your own needs. This can be difficult in relationships. Be sure you communicate to your partner that you are simply taking care of yourself and that this is what you need to do to feel good in the world. Remember however that your partner may be feeling neglected or that you care only for yourself; be sure to communicate this is not the case but that you do need to prioritise your passionate emotional responses and impulses.

Moon in Taurus

In relationships the Moon in Taurus loves stability and preserving a safe environment. A partner who chops and changes or who is very unpredictable simply will not suit you. Be sure to connect with someone who is going to honour your need for a quiet, peaceful life. It is also likely that you are a very tactile person so ensuring your partner understands your need to be touched is very important.

Moon in Gemini

For the Moon in Gemini getting bored in a partnership can be a real problem. Your constant need for new ideas and variety of experience, plus sufficient room to breathe and flit about as you wish to, could be hard for a slower, more stable partner to manage. Take care of your own needs by feeding your soul with communication, books, courses and exposure to new ideas. An intellectual or partner of many interests could suit you very well.

Moon in Cancer

With Moon in Cancer you may become emotionally dependent on another very quickly. It may be important therefore that you do not give away your affections too easily. You require someone who can be sensitive to your emotional needs, and understand that your moods will wax and wane like the Moon herself. It may also be too easy for you to become caught up in your own emotions, to the extent that you are unable to stand back and see the situation from a more detached perspective.

Moon in Leo

Here there is a natural love of playfulness and drama. You need to be appreciated as special and unique. A partner who does not give you sufficient attention as a unique person will not be nourishing for you. Allow yourself to shine and be loved as the queen or king in your relationship, but equally remember to let the spotlight focus on your partner sometimes too. With this Moon-sign you may become self-absorbed without realising it.

Moon in Virgo

This Moon-sign confers a love of order and routine. You like to have an orderly environment, which is clean and efficient, and which feeds your requirement to have things around you which have practical value. A chaotic partner who cannot stick to meeting times or honour your need to be economical and tidy could upset you. Ensuring your partner respects your rituals and routines is very important.

Moon in Libra

With this Moon-sign you may be too prone to taking your partner's needs into consideration and neglecting your own. Your natural instinct is to reach out to the other and you are giving and loving in this regard. However, ultimately you require a partnership of equals and therefore ensuring you find a balance will be the key to emotional happiness in partnership.

Moon in Scorpio

Moon in Scorpio has intense emotional needs, and can be very private and secretive. In relationship you require a partner who can affect you on the deepest levels but who will respect your need to sometimes keep things to yourself. It is very important you have a partner you trust as jealousy and possessiveness can be issues. Ensure you connect with someone who is able to meet your needs on a deep level.

Moon in Sagittarius

With this Moon-sign you must have plenty of space and freedom in your daily life. You are nurtured by your ability to look into the future and dream large dreams. You must have a partner who allows you the room to do this and appreciates that you cannot always be caught up in the mundane realities of day to day existence. A relationship that nurtures your innate optimism and grand ideas will be ideal.

Moon in Capricorn

The Moon in Capricorn generally suggests a very serious individual, who likes a structured, mature relationship that lasts the test of time. It is important that you have a partner who can respect this and take a serious enough approach to your connection. Don't waste time on those who mock your approach or tell you it is too old-fashioned or stiff.

Moon in Aquarius

With this Moon-sign it is important your relationship is an embodiment of your own principles, which are likely to be humane, compassionate and show concern for wider society. Being involved with someone who has no interest beyond themselves would not be nurturing for you. You also require sufficient independence in relationships that you remain your own, rational, detached person so a partner who is very needy or clings to you is unlikely to be suitable.

Moon in Pisces

The Moon in Pisces is a very romantic placement with a strong need to escape on a daily basis. You will love a relationship that allows you to feel at one with your partner and in which you can enjoy escapism together. For example, many movies or a very romantic meal with a glass or two of wine would be very nurturing for you. Also, following some spiritual path together would be a wonderful way of nurturing your Moon-sign.

When you are in a relationship, remember to take into account your partner's Moon-sign as well as your own. They have needs too!

We will now briefly look at the Moon in the houses, in terms of how the placements relate to relationships.

Moon in the 1st House

This is the position of emotional independence, so your feelings will come in to all your actions and beginnings. It may be too easy to focus on your own needs, so ensure you take those of your partner into consideration.

Moon in the 2nd House

There is a powerful need for security here and the more you increase your self-esteem the more nurtured you feel. Ensure your relationships feed your sense of security but be careful not to let focus on your own finances detract from sharing in your partnership.

Moon in the 3rd House

Communication is essential to your way of being. Cultivate open dialogue in your partnerships and ensure you express your feelings. Allow your partner room to talk too though!

Moon in the 4th House

Having a home and domestic environment that nurtures you is key here. Your relationship should feed into this; sharing a home together may be particularly important to you.

Moon in the 5th House

Joy, fun and romance are essential for you. Plan your relationships so there is plenty of social time and enjoyment. Take holidays together or start joint hobbies.

Moon in the 6th House

Ensure your relationship fits into your beloved rituals and routines. However do not be so attached to them that you cannot see beyond them. They may alienate your partner if they are too rigid.

Moon in the 7th House

Here emotional need for a partner is great. Cultivate a stable relationship that allows you to feel safe and nurtured. But beware of your tendency to become too emotionally dependent.

Moon in the 8th House

Allow yourself to find a relationship that is sufficiently intense and engaging on an emotional level. Let it take you to the deeper places you crave.

Moon in the 9th House

Let your relationships take you to new places, both literal and metaphorical. Travel and explore the grand ideas of the world. A mundane partnership is not for you.

Moon in the 10th House

Allow the nurturing you find in your career to support you in your relationships. You want a connection that enhances your status and supports your ambitions in the world.

Moon in the 11th House

You require friendship on an emotional level. With your partner join groups and be known as the couple who socialise together.

Moon in the 12th House

You require time alone so make sure your partner understands this and gives you the space you need. Find nurturing in meditation and quiet time. Ensure you have a partner who shares your spiritual understanding of life.

Now we have collated information on the Moon in each sign and house, in terms of how it may play out in relationship, we can attempt to synthesise the interpretations, to look at a specific Moon placement. From the examples below you should be able to write an interpretation for your own Moon placement.

Moon in Leo in the 6th House

The Moon in Leo needs to shine and feel special in its relationships, and in the 6th house this will particularly play out at work and in daily routines and rituals. A relationship that puts glamour and glitz into everyday life would suit this individual well.

Moon in Capricorn in the 2nd House

The Moon in Capricorn loves a serious, mature committed relationship. In the 2nd house this Moon needs to feel very secure, particularly financially. It does not however like to feel dependent, for what is important here is feeling supported by one's own resources. Any relationship therefore must honour this individual's strong need for self-sufficiency, which is shown by the Moon in Capricorn and its placement in the 2nd house. Shared financial arrangements may need particularly clear handling.

Moon in Sagittarius in the 5th House

The Moon in Sagittarius needs a relationship that will honour its growth and need to constantly see new possibilities. In the 5th house this Moon also has a strong need for self-expression and creative outlets. Any relationship must contain sufficient room for these instincts to express; this is likely to involve time alone and an understanding from the partner that this individual must have plenty of room to visualise their future.

Moon in Taurus in the 7th House

This Moon will love the stability and security of partnership and may see their partner as the one who can provide this. Whilst any relationship will need a solid and stable form to keep this individual happy, it will ideally also provide a structure whereby the individual can start to realise their own potential for building resources and finding a firm base from which to live.

Moon in Aquarius in the 9th House

The Moon in Aquarius will need much space and independence within a relationship, particularly when it comes to their love of higher knowledge, of exploring grand philosophies and ideas about life and the world. A relationship will need to have room to allow this individual to soar up into lofty realms of thought.

Honouring the needs of your Moon could not be more important. Ensure your relationship allows you space to be yourself, and you will have created an excellent structure within which to continue your connection with your soul-mate.

Chapter 13

Assembling your unique Relationship Needs profile

E HAVE NOW COVERED THE areas of the astrological chart that show our core relationship needs—our Descendant sign, our Venus, the 7th house and the Moon. We are therefore ready to assemble our own relationship needs profile.

We will use the following template. The keyword glossary from chapter 8 may be used here for ease of reference. You may however simply wish to look back to the descriptions of each of your unique placements. You can add as much detail as you like to the basic template; the idea is to build up a sense of what your real needs in relationship are so that you are aware of them when you meet your soul-mate and go about establishing a relationship that meets the requirements of your own soul.

My approach to life is [insert qualities of Ascendant sign]. In other people I am therefore prone to seeking [insert qualities of Descendant sign]. Seeking these qualities in myself may help me in my quest for a soul-mate.

The style of relationship I enjoy is [insert Venus sign qualities]. A particular area of life that I enjoy exploring with my partner is [insert Venus house life areas].

In relationship I may be prone to exploring issues connected with [insert issues of 7th house planets, if any]. These are qualities I may 'give away' to another and it is therefore important for me to find them just for myself.

My emotional needs in relationship are [insert qualities of Moon-sign]. To feel nurtured with another I particularly need support in the area of [insert house placement of the Moon].

We can now run through a few examples.

Suppose a person has the Ascendant in Cancer, Descendant in Capricorn, Venus in Capricorn, the Sun and Venus in the 7th house, and the Moon in Gemini in the 12th house.

Their unique relationship profile would look something like the following:

My approach to life is sensitive, imaginative and emotional. In other people I am therefore prone to seeking stability, longevity and seriousness. Seeking these qualities in myself may help me in my quest for a soul-mate.

The style of relationship I enjoy is serious, mature and committed. A particular area of life that I enjoy exploring with my partner is equality and partnership.

In relationship I may be prone to exploring issues connected with my identity and values. These are qualities I may 'give away' to another and it is therefore important for me to find them just for myself.

My emotional needs in relationship are mental stimulation, space and variety. To feel nurtured with another I particularly need support in the area of quiet time alone and spiritual connection.

From this profile, we see this is someone who has a particular focus on relationships and those of a serious, committed style in particular. This could result in someone who engages in a long-term partnership quite easily and perhaps identifies with that relationship very strongly. However, we note that the lunar needs are very much connected with needing time alone and space for spiritual connection. There might therefore be a conflict here. This individual may need to be careful to construct a life whereby space and time alone can be found whilst also engaging in an important partnership for the long-term.

As another example we could take a man with Scorpio rising, Taurus on the Descendant, Venus in Sagittarius, Chiron in the 7th house and the Moon in Aries in the 5th house.

His profile would look something like this:

My approach to life is deep, intense and probing. In other people I am therefore prone to seeking stability, security and simplicity. Seeking these qualities in myself may help me in my quest for a soul-mate.

The style of relationship I enjoy is friendly, expansive and freedom-orientated. A particular area of life that I enjoy exploring with my partner is earning power and self-esteem.

In relationship I may be prone to exploring issues connected with wisdom and healing. These are qualities I may 'give away' to another and it is therefore important for me to find them just for myself.

My emotional needs in relationship are for action, adventure and dynamism. To feel nurtured with another I particularly need support in the area of romance, play and recreation.

This is a man who needs a stable partnership but who also has a great deal of energy for an expansive and adventurous partnership that allows him to be creative and self-expressive. Yet he also has an eye on earning, perhaps through the inspiration of a partner.

It will be important for him to find a relationship that allows for this dual function of expansion, excitement and creativity whilst also having quite a practical side, which allows him to focus on his finances in tandem with a partner. There is also something about finding wisdom or healing through partnership and before he can engage with another he may need to deal with his own sense of pain or fears about rejection from others.

Our last example will be a woman who has Leo rising, Aquarius on the Descendant, Venus in Virgo in the 2nd house, no planets in the 7th and Moon in Gemini in the 10th house. Her profile would look something like this:

My approach to life is proud, dramatic and creative. In other people I am therefore prone to seeking tolerance, compassion and open-mindedness.

The style of relationship I enjoy is precise, exacting and intelligent. A particular area of life that I enjoy exploring with my partner is earning power and self-esteem.

My emotional needs in relationship are for mental stimulation, social contacts and many interests. To feel nurtured with another I particularly need support in the area of career, status and public life.

There are two indications here of relationships being connected with earning power and career and therefore this woman may be prone to meeting her soul-mates through working situations or business ventures. She also has a lot of emphasis on intelligence within relationship and a relationship that allows bold, bright public expression (Leo rising and Moon in the 10th house). She will therefore require a soul-mate with whom she can relate on an intellectual level and whom does not hold her back from shining out there in the public eye.

With an understanding of our true self and also now our relationship profile, we are now ready to move on to the last part of finding a soul-mate with astrology.

Part 4

Putting it All Together

We have now come far on our journey. You have discovered important information about yourself and how you can enhance your happiness and fulfilment as an individual. You will also have discovered and reflected upon your own relationship needs as shown by the astrological chart. Bearing all this in mind, and continuing to fully engage with your own path to fulfilment at all times, you may also now be ready to consider calling your soul-mate. In chapter 14 we will discuss how you might attract in that partner and in chapter 15 we will explore questions that relate to soul-mates and relationships.

Chapter 14

Calling your Soul-Mate

You have already done a lot of work on calling your soul-mate. Even in growing your awareness and expanding your understanding of who you really are, you have put yourself in a better place in which to attract in the perfect partner for your current level of growth. It may therefore be that you have already met that special person!

If you have not however, there are additional actions you can take to improve your chances of meeting a soul-mate.

Cutting past ties

Firstly, it is most important that you cut the ties you have to any old relationships. This does not necessarily mean cutting them out of your life altogether (although it might). What it does however mean is that you need to take a very honest look at your life and consider where past relationships and ties could be holding you back from moving forwards and meeting someone new.

Even if you are not 'in a relationship' with an ex-partner, if you are still involved in any 'messy' emotional involvement with them, you will have energetic ties that are blocking you from moving forward. This is particularly the case in sexual matters. It can be only too tempting to sleep with an ex- partner, husband or wife. This is someone who you know, whose body you are familiar with, and who may seem like a 'safe bet' to release sexual and emotional tension or feelings of loneliness.

However, when you have sexual relations with another human being, powerful psychic and emotional ties are activated. Your energies become blurred and mixed together. If you are serious about finding a new love in your life, you must avoid falling into the past in this manner. Realise that it is in your very best interests to go forward and allow yourself to meet your new partner with your energy intact!

To release energetic ties it is very helpful not only to enforce the physical practice of keeping boundaries between yourself and old partners, but also to undertake a meditation whereby you meet the other person, say what you need to say and then cut the cords of energy between you.

Imagine beams of light linking you and the other person; take an imaginary sword and at the right moment, cut the beams, leaving both of you free. Then surround yourself in white or gold light to heal any wounds caused by the cutting of the ties.

This process will not dissolve any genuine ties of love between you, love that is based on two adults mutually respecting and relating to each other from genuine places of respective individuality. If however you find that after completing this exercise there appear to be very strong ties of love and powerful attraction between you, then you may wish to reassess whether this partner is really someone you want as an 'ex'. It could be that this is your new soul-mate too! Be careful here though, because unless both or one of you have significantly changed and grown to the same level as the other since you parted, it may be quite likely that the problems of the relationship will resurface at some point.

Once you have dealt with any old, lingering relationships that may be preventing you from moving forward, you are now ready to consider actively calling your soul-mate towards you. Before you do that however, there may be one last piece of preparatory work you might wish to do. This involves ensuring your 'male' and 'female' halves are in balance.

Owning our 'Male' and 'Female' halves

Regardless of our own gender we each have an inner male and an inner female. The psychologist Carl Jung gave the terms 'animus' and 'anima' to these two inner characters. The inner male represents the qualities within us of assertion, dynamism, leadership, rational and logical analysis, and an outwards orientation towards life. The inner female represents the more flowing, intuitive side of our being, the part that is naturally connected to the creative and imaginative realms.

We might also think of these two beings as connected with the right and left sides of the brain. Often the left side of the brain is thought of as the logical, rational side, whereas the right side is the more creative and intuitive.

How can you be sure these two parts of yourself are in balance? One way is to undertake a meditation to try and contact each of these figures, an inner male and an inner female. Imagine you are in a sacred space, somewhere meaningful to you, perhaps a forest with a clearing, a beautiful garden or landscape. Then visualise a doorway of some kind, perhaps the entrance to an old mysterious tree, the mouth of a cave, or an actual doorway to a hut. In turn see your inner male and inner female step out of the entrance and imagine a conversation you might have with them. Then, be sure to visualise yourself merging with each of the figures so that you really own each side of your being.

Being in balance with both male and female halves puts you in a strong position from which to meet your soul-mate. This is because you will be approaching life from a place of wholeness and you will not be seeking a partner to fill a gap. For example, if a woman is not sufficiently in touch with her inner male, she may play the role of the 'helpless female' needing assistance with anything remotely logical or practical. Yet often, if she takes the time to look within, she will find she has plenty of skills of her own that she may previously have projected onto male people in her life. Taking back the projection, which means we do not see people so much as mirrors of ourselves but who they really are, allows us to relate from a place of greater authenticity.

Calling Your Soul-Mate

Once you are satisfied that the male and female halves within you are in balance, you are now ready to call your soul-mate. It is advisable to undertake some particular ritual to do this, as this will ingrain the belief in your mind and heart that you are now ready to meet someone who is just right for you. You may undertake a meditation, and imagine yourself calling out to your soul-mate, like a wolf howling into the night or a whale sending out a signal far into the vast ocean waves. Or you may wish to construct your own ritual, perhaps lighting some candles, and making your own prayers to call in a person. You might also wish to try writing down all the qualities you want in a soul-mate and then burning the paper as part of your calling ritual.

Whatever process you choose to call-in your soul-mate it is important that you are then able to let your prayer go out into the universe, to release it. By working on yourself and your own happiness, you should have plenty to keep you occupied until you meet the person in question. As you move through daily life, keep asking yourself, am I being who I really am, and fully expressing myself? The more you do this and stay in harmony with your own self and desires, the more likely you will meet someone uniquely suitable for you.

After you have released your prayer or request you must have faith. As we live in a friendly, conscious universe, you will obtain what you have requested, as long as you are open to receiving. Be expectant, but not desperate. Desperation is a quality that repels, so be happy as you are, whilst knowing that a happy, loving relationship is on its way to find you.

Should you take specific action to find your soul-mate?

Being passive and waiting for Mr or Mrs Right to walk into your life may work, and it may not. There is a secret to taking action, which goes like this. Once you align yourself with who you really are, with the help of astrology, and raise awareness of what your relationship needs are, again through astrology, you will be living in harmony with the universe. In this state of harmony you will be inspired to take certain actions over others.

Therefore, you should not take forced action to find your soul-mate. If social opportunities arise or dating websites or other avenues appear in your life check in with your intuition. Does it feel right to pursue this particular social activity? Or this particular dating website? If it does then this may be part of the magical journey the universe is offering you in order to find your soul-mate. If it does not let it go and wait until the right opportunity comes along. Keep your eyes and ears open; listen to the signs that appear in your life, and follow the omens that seem to be lining the path. Taking action is a good thing, but only if it is inspired action. And the route to inspired action is to be in tune with yourself, as we have been discussing throughout this book.

Following a Passion

There is however one type of action that you may pursue without concern, and this is the exploration of any deeply held desire that you have. This does not have to be connected with a relationship or a soul-mate, and in fact it is often better if it is not. Think back to any dream or passion you had as a child or at any previous age which you have never had the opportunity to fulfil. Remember the longings of your soul. This might be learning a particular language, playing a musical instrument, visiting a certain country or many other desires. It does not matter what exactly it is; what matters is that this desire is unique to you and is something that you feel drawn to.

Next, follow that desire. Enrol for that language class or a lesson or two on the piano; arrange a holiday to that destination you always longed to go to. The desires of the soul are very powerful indeed. It does not matter if they seem unrelated to anything in your life or history. The fact that something captures your interest suggests it is important to your own journey. In pursuing this passion you will take a step in the right direction to meeting your soul-mate. The desires within us must be honoured. So take time out to reflect on all those things that used to seem so fascinating and reawaken some of that magic now. Follow the dream and you may be surprised at what or whom you meet along the way! Desire, like love, is the language of the soul.

Loving Yourself

Lastly, but by no means least, it is extremely important to love yourself, to have a healthy sense of self-esteem. If you are honouring your astrological energy pattern you will be making some positive steps towards this but you can also take more direct action. Louise Hay has long recommended mirror work, facing yourself in the mirror and telling yourself that you love and approve of your own being. This should be said in the form 'I love and approve of myself' as she recommends. Positive mantras like this one can never be said too many times; self-love forms the basis of a happy life on many levels.

The importance of self-care cannot be underestimated. You cannot expect another human being to love you if you do not love yourself. The world is a mirror so the more you honour and value yourself, the more others in your life will do the same. Take time out for pampering and allow yourself a break from your responsibilities and duties.

You should now be in an optimal frame of mind in which to meet your soul-mate. With constant attention to your authenticity, acting on inspiration and intuition, having cut any old unhealthy ties and balanced your inner male and female, following the passions of your soul, and loving yourself at all stages, it is only a matter of time before your soul-mate appears. Enjoy!

Chapter 15

Happy Ever After?

O NCE YOU HAVE MET A soul-mate your work continues! The beginning of a new relationship is just that, a beginning. You must not forget what you have learnt about yourself thus far. Being true to oneself whilst also maintaining a close, loving relationship with another human being is one of the hardest tasks in life. Or at least, if may take some consideration and effort to really get it right.

You should never forget that you are an individual. Your partner, no matter how much you love them, is separate from you. They cannot provide the meaning or happiness in your life. Happiness comes from within you, and although this may increase by the existence of a loving relationship, it should never be the only source of happiness in your life. If it is, the relationship may be a dangerously dependent one, with you having to compromise on vital elements of your own nature because you become afraid that the relationship will not work out.

Communication

Communication is essential to a good relationship. Express your feelings and share them with your partner on a regular basis. Try to cut out conversations that use phrases such as 'You are...' Instead start from 'I'. So instead of saying, 'You make me feel unloved and unappreciated' you might say 'I feel unappreciated when you take the meals I prepare for granted or do not notice when I have made a special effort to dress-up'. This allows the other person to respond more freely, and less defensively, and is sure to open up better channels of communication.

When a Problem Arises, Look to Yourself

Another good strategy in working at your relationship is to always look to your own self and behaviour when a problem arises. If you feel your partner is not giving you enough attention, ask whether you are giving them enough attention. Making a few small changes in how you relate to them could have a big impact on how they relate to you. Your relationship is a co-created field of energy between you and when you make a change, they also have to change—that's the energetic law! Thus the more you change yourself, the more your partner will change. If there is genuine love between you, and you are changing and growing for the better, it is highly likely your partner will also change and grow for the better.

Time as a Couple

Making time for you both as a couple is also very important. If you have busy careers, or children to look after, it can be all too easy to forget the first flush of magic that existed between you at the beginning of the relationship and to make time for just you two. Sometimes, with modern life being as busy as it is, it may be necessary to actually make a firm date each week with each other, an evening or period of time that is just for you. Perhaps you can go out for a meal, spend time together in the beauties of nature, or just curl up together at home. The important thing is complete attention on the other person, without the distraction of work, hobbies or children.

Forever After?

Relationships do not always last forever, but you have a good chance of a lasting, committed connection the more each of you is aware of your own needs as an individual, and the more each of you is prepared to let the other be totally themselves. It can sometimes be that life events or experiences are so extreme that one of you is pulled into a period of rapid growth which leaves the other behind, or which has seen them grow in another direction. In this situation it may sometimes be that the relationship has come to an end and that you would both be happier and more fulfilled taking new directions. The ending of a relationship is not a failure, and neither does it mean that this was not a soul-mate. A soul-mate is someone very special who comes into your life for a period of time. That time may often be many years, even decades, but it could be shorter. None of us knows the exact weave of our fate, and we must be open to change and growth as we traverse the journey of life.

Ending a Relationship

With this proviso however, the step of ending a relationship is a big decision to make and may often be unnecessary. If you are unhappy it is likely to be connected to a feeling of not being able to express yourself. If you are afraid of expressing yourself as you really are because you think your partner will not approve or will criticise you then this means you are operating from fear. Put fear aside, because often a fear about what your partner may or may not do is all in your own head. All you can do is be yourself, and ensure you love your partner to the best of your ability. Some compromise will always be necessary in a relationship, but this should not be a compromise of your essential self.

More than one Soul-Mate?

Is it possible that we have more than one soul-mate? I believe the answer to this is yes. A soul-mate is a special soul, linked to your own, that at a certain time in your life provides a very close match to your level of growth and awareness. There is a good chance that in the universe of human beings, more than one person will fit this profile. Some soul-mate relationships may have been contracted for a finite time before we entered this incarnation; this may often be the case where fate seems to intervene and split two people apart who were clearly soul-mates.

We simply cannot know, unless we have special psychic powers, about the contracts or agreements we made prior to entering this incarnation. We can only do our best in the place we find ourselves, and understand that at any point of our life it is possible to find a new soul-mate, and to again find happiness in relationship.

Happy Alone?

There may of course come a time when you do not wish to meet anybody new. If you feel perfectly happy alone then there is absolutely nothing wrong with that. In fact, the message of this book from the beginning has been that the priority for each of us is to express who we really are. We do not have to have a soul-mate in order to do that. Honouring one's own heart, and one's own soul, is what needs to come first. Soul-mates may come, and they may go. As long as we each continue on our Royal Road, which is the highest expression of our potential in this life, we know we are where we need to be on life's highway.

About the Author

LAURA ANDRIKOPOULOS is an astrologer from Birmingham, England. She is a prize-winning holder of the Diploma of the Faculty of Astrological Studies and is currently President of that School. Laura holds degrees in Mathematics, Theology and an MA in Cultural Astronomy & Astrology. She is particularly interested in using astrology to facilitate awareness and personal growth, thereby enriching all areas of our lives. Her website is www.starpoetry.co.uk.